"Peace is a troubling tension: r_____ justice; reparations call for ac_____ that can never be undone. Mic_____ people trying to live truthfully _____ are not neutral stories: they are stories of opinions, hopes, _____, demands, and anxieties. To read them is to be brought into the complication of enmity, restoration, and true living. This book is a muscle, an ache, a practice of asking the troubling questions at the heart of peace."

PÁDRAIG Ó TUAMA, poet, theologian, and host of *Poetry Unbound* with the On Being Project

"Not many people get argued into thinking differently, but lots of people get 'storied' into thinking differently. Sometimes our hearts move first and our heads follow. Michael McRay is a care-taker of stories, and he's a master at it. He handles some of the most delicate stories in the world with the care they deserve and offers them to us as a holy sacrament. Let these stories move you, disturb you, shape you, and challenge you to change the world so that the generations to come read history as a love story."

SHANE CLAIBORNE, author, speaker, activist, and cofounder of Red Letter Christians

"Michael McRay gets poignantly to the heart of the matter. This is a book about the varied faces of grief, love, and reconciliation. It is incisive, smart, and acutely necessary for our times."

COLUM MCCANN, author of *Apeirogon* and winner of the National Book Award

"Michael McRay offers us the collective testimony of people across the world whose stories rebuke cheap reconciliation and challenge us to aim for more. In *I Am Not Your Enemy*, I hear the yearning for hope grounded in truth. McRay's truth-telling makes room for us to see ourselves—and to see beyond ourselves. Truth-telling and hopefulness work together in these stories, igniting power in the least likely people to stretch for a world they haven't seen but know is possible."

EMMA JORDAN-SIMPSON, executive director of Fellowship of Reconcilia-tion USA

"This timely book is driven by goodwill and belief in human dignity. Michael McRay brilliantly weaves together stories of people involved in different conflicts. With a great inquiring spirit, he wrestles with difficult questions that are significant to all those working for justice. Read this book and be moved to tears, yet also inspired by hope."

RAJA SHEHADEH, lawyer and author of *Going Home* and *Palestinian Walks*

"A stunning book of compelling stories from divided societies, each endowed with a powerful message of hope. Michael McRay finds meaning within chaos and helps us get our bearings when feeling lost or overwhelmed by the work we need to do in the world. His powerful writing allows us the privilege of feeling compassion instead of fear, inspiration in the midst of despair, and harmony in the midst of division. Seekers of justice can use these stories like a map of love."

BECCA STEVENS, founder of Thistle Farms and author of *Love Heals*

"Michael McRay invites us to peer into the challenges of social healing and reconciliation in tough places and tough times. To read this book is to arrive quickly at the realization that these stories are about us, about the places we live, and the neighbors we have. They are about how we choose to show up in the midst of fear and division, espousing the fundamental belief that we are called to love our enemies. A more timely set of stories can hardly be imagined."

JOHN PAUL LEDERACH, international peacebuilder and professor emeritus at the Kroc Institute for International Peace Studies at the University of Notre Dame

"Michael McRay finds hope where most people have given up long ago. He reminds us that there is love and humanity everywhere, even in the most unlikely places. As a peacebuilder and citizen of the deeply divided country of Bosnia-Herzegovina, I know firsthand the necessity of McRay's stories and wisdom. There are ways out of the old logic of enemies. This book, at its best, shows us how."

ZANA MARJANOVIĆ, actress, filmmaker, and former member of the Parliament of the Federation of Bosnia and Herzegovina

"In our era of fake news, hate speech, xenophobia, and racism, Michael McRay offers a compelling way back to dignity and self-respect—by choosing to listen carefully to the stories of so-called enemies instead of showering them with fear and prejudice. Through the process of storytelling, McRay shows that our enemies may be transformed into partners for a better world. This is a book that should be taken very seriously indeed."

FANIE DU TOIT, senior advisor of the Institute for Justice and Reconciliation in Cape Town, South Africa

"Michael McRay understands the power of story to transform how we envision and relate to the world. With grace and humility, his book seeks a new narrative to stitch together a world that seems increasingly divided even as it becomes smaller, more interrelated, and more accessible than ever."

PAMELA OLSON, author of *Fast Times in Palestine*

"Michael McRay has a sharp ability to immerse himself in areas of conflict and then bring the experience to life in writing. McRay does this not only by describing historical events in detail, but by reflecting deeply on the feelings, thoughts, and insights of the people living within intense intractable conflict."

SALIM MUNAYER, director of Musalaha ministry of reconciliation in Jerusalem

"In this important book, Michael McRay says he did not write to make a living off other people's stories. This makes the book already a rare thing—the author respects and shares in the suffering of those about which the stories are told. For readers, he weaves a framework in which we find more life for ourselves. McRay is a truthful, caring, and inspirational guide to rethinking the stories that imprison us and reimagining ones that could set us free."

GARETH HIGGINS, founder of *The Porch Magazine* and Movies & Meaning and cofounder of the Wild Goose Festival and New Story Festival

"These are stories that have traveled continents, written in the tears of others, inviting us to listen. When heard, they return us to listening in the places we now call home to the pain we must articulate and answer if we too are to take part in the great work of healing-justice."

JARROD MCKENNA, founding director of the First Home Project and co-host of *InVerse Podcast*

"Michael McRay walks directly into areas where fierce enmities have been nurtured for decades or even centuries and shares stories of healing, reconciliation, and hope. His work can help you see your enemies in a humane new light and learn how to resist the push to create enemies in the first place. These stories of rehumanization, justice, and reconciliation are perfect for our times."

KARLA MCLAREN, author of *The Art of Empathy* and *The Language of Emotions*

"This book is a timely illustration of the human spirit craving liberation, justice, dignity, and equality. Michael McRay brings to life the reasons that dialogue should be used as a tool to drive tremendous change to improve the world, and takes us on an unforgettable journey through the Holy Land, Ireland, and South Africa."

SAMAR ALI, founding president of Millions of Conversations

I AM NOT YOUR ENEMY

Stories to Transform a Divided World

I AM
NOT
YOUR
ENEMY

MICHAEL T. MCRAY

Foreword by Ishmael Beah

bestselling author of *A Long Way Gone*

**Herald
P R E S S**

Harrisonburg, Virginia

Also by Michael T. McRay

Keep Watch with Me, with Claire Brown
Where the River Bends
Letters from "Apartheid Street"

Herald Press
PO Box 866, Harrisonburg, Virginia 22803
www.HeraldPress.com

Library of Congress Cataloging-in-Publication Data
Names: McRay, Michael T., author.
Title: I am not your enemy : stories to transform a divided world / Michael
 T. McRay.
Description: Harrisonburg, Virginia : Herald Press, 2020. | Includes
 bibliographical references.
Identifiers: LCCN 2019044201 (print) | LCCN 2019044202 (ebook) | ISBN
 9781513805931 (paperback) | ISBN 9781513805948 (hardcover) | ISBN
 9781513805955 (ebook)
Subjects: LCSH: Conduct of life. | Interpersonal relations. | Peace. |
 Nonviolence.
Classification: LCC BJ1597 .M37 2020 (print) | LCC BJ1597 (ebook) | DDC
 170/.44--dc23
LC record available at https://lccn.loc.gov/2019044201
LC ebook record available at https://lccn.loc.gov/2019044202

Published in association with The Christopher Ferebee Agency,
www.christopherferebee.com.

I AM NOT YOUR ENEMY
© 2020 by Michael T. McRay. Released by Herald Press, Harrisonburg, Virginia
 22803. 800-245-7894.
All rights reserved.
Library of Congress Control Number: 2019044201
International Standard Book Number: 978-1-5138-0593-1 (paperback);
 978-1-5138-0594-8 (hardcover); 978-1-5138-0595-5 (ebook)
Printed in United States of America
Cover and interior design by Reuben Graham

Scripture quotations in this publication are from the *Common English Bible*.
Copyright 2011 by the Common English Bible. All rights reserved. Used by permission. (www.CommonEnglishBible.com)

24 23 22 21 20   10 9 8 7 6 5 4 3 2 1

To Brittany, my music—
it's in your shelter that I make my home.
I love you, and that's it.
Forever.

To be hopeful in bad times is not . . . foolishly romantic. It is based on the fact that human history is a history not only of cruelty, but also of compassion, sacrifice, courage, kindness. What we choose to emphasize in this complex history will determine our lives.

—*Howard Zinn,*
You Can't Be Neutral on a Moving Train

CONTENTS

FOREWORD

One of the most powerful weapons we use to dehumanize each other is the stories we believe about the other,
and especially those stories that are built on fear. Such stories
become fossilized in our minds and bodies to the point that
we forget that stories are medicine meant to remind us that
we belong to each other. More so now than ever, we need
such stories "to save us from our fear," as Michael T. McRay
explains through stories of the other in this important, timely,
and needed book, *I Am Not Your Enemy*.

This book is filled with deep, insightful encounters and
conversations with remarkable individuals in Israel, Palestine, Northern Ireland, and South Africa, people who know
conflict, injustice, violence, and dehumanization only too
well. In it, McRay explores the need to embark on the difficult but necessary road of reconciliation, seeking truth in the

stories of others so that fear is replaced with empathy. This path may be one way to begin to regain our wavering belief in the sacrosanct nature of all life, no matter where we live. Even, and perhaps especially, here in the United States, where violence is on the rise and few spaces exist for those who tell differing stories to meet, the medicine of these stories can help us heal.

I know firsthand about conflict and the violence it begets, having endured a brutal civil war in Sierra Leone during my childhood. I also know about reconciliation and forgiveness, those lofty words that are easily asked of those who live in dehumanizing contexts. Through this book, we learn of the possibility of peace and of the practical requirements of forgiveness and reconciliation. Can you reconcile while injustice continues? Can you forgive those who burned down your home while still living in its ruins? When and how do we become someone else's enemy? And how can that enmity be undone? Attempting to answer these questions is itself an act of offering medicine to the world.

Some years ago, I had the remarkable privilege of attending a lecture by Desmond Tutu at the New York University School of Law. He told the following story about the dilemma of reconciliation. "Once upon a time, there was a family that owned a bicycle, and it was their livelihood. The father used it to get to work on time and to take his children to school. The mother used it to go to the market. Then one morning the bicycle went missing, and the family began to suffer. Their life deteriorated. Time passed and there was a knock on their door. The father opened the door and there stood one of their neighbors with the bicycle. 'I am truly sorry for what I did. Will you forgive me?' he asked. The father agreed with a nod, eyeing the bicycle. 'Thank you,' said the neighbor. He turned around and left with the bicycle. What it will take not to chase him down in that moment is where the change lies."[1]

I have thought about this story many times as an illustration of selflessness in undoing the cycle of violence. When you embark on reconciliation, you might not get what you lost. Regardless, you seek to create a possibility to begin anew in how you see those who have been your enemy. If we succeed in listening to the truth that lies beyond the propaganda that makes us enemies, then perhaps we will begin to see that we are not enemies at all. McRay, in this book, has prepared the path for us to begin that journey by finding wisdom again in stories rather than fear.

—*Ishmael Beah*
Author of *A Long Way Gone: Memoirs of a Boy Soldier*, *Radiance of Tomorrow: A Novel*, and *Little Family: A Novel*

---

1. Desmond Tutu, "Desmond Tutu Discusses Addressing the Past" (lecture, New York University School of Law, New York, NY, October 23, 2006). In sharing this story, Tutu, an outspoken advocate for reconciliation and reparations, was by no means advocating disingenuous requests for forgiveness. Rather, the story speaks to the deep and challenging work of ending cycles of violence.

INTRODUCTION

We need saving.

We fear each other. We fear people who don't look like us, don't think like us, don't live near us, don't talk like us. Democrats think Republicans are dangerous, and Republicans see the same threat in Dems. We spray-paint hate speech on each other's houses, rip hijabs and turbans off each other's heads, attack one another with bombs at concerts and with cars on bridges, shoot each other in nightclubs and malls and schools, threaten each other in our places of worship, watch quietly as cops kill unarmed black people and suffer no consequences, attack police with hammers and guns, yell vile insults from our cars, demand Mexicans "go home" after we've eaten in their restaurants, and cry over the drowned body of a Syrian child yet deny refuge to the rest of his family. The list goes on and on and on.

We've forgotten—or perhaps never really learned—how to live together well. Like many people, I am often tempted to believe there's no hope for us.

But I can't. I believe there *is* hope. We can be saved from this madness.

And *we* are the ones who can save ourselves.

That's why I wrote this book—to remind us of what we can be with one another.

To remind us of *who* we can be with one another.

THERE'S A CURIOUS STORY about Jesus in the eighth chapter of Mark's gospel. The writer says Jesus and those with him come to a village called Bethsaida, and the locals bring him a man who is blind and wanting sight. But Jesus doesn't grant the man sight on the spot; instead, he takes him out of the village and—strangely enough—spits in his eyes.

In the previous chapter, Jesus spit when he was healing someone who couldn't hear or speak. Now he's spitting for someone who can't see. Sometimes I wonder if Jesus just needed to mix up his healing routine a bit and thought spitting could be a nice change of pace. Whatever the reason, after spitting in the man's eyes, Jesus puts his hands on them and asks the man what he sees. The man says he can see people walking around, but they look like trees. I imagine it was blurry, like a camera out of focus. Jesus quits spitting and touches the man's eyes again. Like magic, his sight is clear. The text says the man "looked with his eyes wide open."

I don't know why Jesus spits, and I don't know why he has to touch the man's eyes twice to heal him. But I wonder if the writer is telling us that sometimes, change comes in steps.

WAKING UP ON NOVEMBER 9, 2016, many of us in the United States felt bewildered, not recognizing the country we live in. How did someone like Donald Trump win the presidency? How could the United States have allowed—or encouraged—someone like Trump to come to power, a person who espoused racist ideas, openly mocked people groups and individuals, and made sexist and misogynistic comments? Many people felt scared; they still do. Lots of us feel as if we're spinning around, looking for signs that all isn't lost. As I see it, we're waking up, even if slowly. To put it another way, we've had the spit put in our eyes, and we're seeing more than we did before, though it's all still blurry. We're waiting, maybe even searching, for what will open our eyes the rest of the way. And it *will* happen—just as it did for the blind man from Bethsaida. The question is, who will touch our eyes that second time? What will we see when our vision is clear? And how will we know how to make sense of what we see?

That's where the stories in this book come in.

A few years ago, I traveled throughout Israel, Palestine, Northern Ireland, and South Africa. I interviewed more than fifty people about reconciliation, forgiveness, injustice, trauma, and living in divided societies. I went to these places because I saw, more clearly than I had before, the deep divisions in my own country. As a peacebuilding student, teacher, and aspiring practitioner, I wanted to listen to people who have been born into divided societies and are finding ways to live together without violence.

This project was all about learning. I did not intend to write a book; the project was designed and funded as an educational collaboration with Texas Christian University. But as I listened to the wisdom and stories of the remarkable people I met, I knew I wanted to share what I was learning.

The ethics of a project like this are not uncomplicated. Writing other people's stories is like walking through a minefield. This is especially true when you're a white man like me, because white men have profited for a long time by stealing stories from other people and capitalizing on the power of those narratives. I'm writing this book as fully aware as I hope I can be of such complications, and I acknowledge the pitfalls upfront. There is no way to do this type of thing perfectly. My hope is that I've done it with as little harm as possible.

I'm not writing this book to make a living off other people's stories. Writing has never been a bill-paying venture for me, and it won't become one now. I believe in the power of the stories I encountered on my travels, and I want to share some of what I learned. It would feel irresponsible to keep it to myself. Each person I spoke with knew the parameters of the project and that I was recording what they said. Some of the people I spoke with were happy for their stories to be used in the classroom but did not want to appear in a book. I have respected that, and you will not read any of those stories here. Each story that appears in this book appears with the expressed consent of the person I spoke with. Since I recorded every conversation I had during my travels, the quotations from each person are nearly verbatim, with a few minor edits made for the sake of readability at the request of my editor. As much as I can, I'm sharing with you their stories in their own words. Occasionally, I've had to summarize sections simply to keep within word count restrictions. I sent each person the chapter containing their story to elicit feedback and ensure they recognized themselves in my writing and approved. Additionally, I offered honoraria from my book advance to each person whose story appears here, and am donating part of the proceeds to the three major organizations with whom I partnered while traveling. I believe this is good narrative practice, though I'm sure it doesn't eliminate all risks involved with this type of project. Still, I hope this book honors the stories I encountered and those to whom they belong.

Finally, given the locations and demographics of the people I met, I need also to acknowledge the following: I am a white American Christian man. I am many other things as well of course, but I'm naming these because they are particularly relevant. Those identifiers mean I walk with much unearned privilege. That's not to say I haven't worked hard and earned many things in my life. But it is to say that to earn those things, I've not had to overcome racism, sexism, xenophobia, or discrimination because of my religious heritage.

Among other things, to grow up white is to grow up inundated and influenced by white supremacy and racism, particularly anti-black racism. Among other things, to grow up male is to grow up inundated and influenced by sexism and patriarchy. Among other things, to grow up Christian is to grow up within a history and culture of anti-Semitism. It is not possible to escape the conscious and subconscious effects of these oppressions. In my efforts to be a responsible human and to perpetuate as little harm as possible, I am continually reeducating, retraining, and rewiring myself to unlearn these oppressions and remove them from my body, thinking, and language to the fullest extent possible. That being said, this journey is a long one, and I always have more to learn.

I BELIEVE SOME OF THE HIGHEST goals of storytelling, of crafting narratives about our lives, should be cultivating empathy and telling the truth in service of reconciling relationships. Stories are powerful, muscular devices. Storytelling can transform us, whether toward better or worse versions of ourselves. The stories we tell and the ones we listen to change us all the time, in large and little ways, and we'd do well to consider carefully which stories win our attention.

There's a particularly wise book called *In the Shelter*, written by Irish poet and theologian Pádraig Ó Tuama. Pádraig is a friend of mine. He is a lover of words, the stories they make, and the stories behind the words that make the stories. In one section of his book, he explores the etymology of the word *story*: "The history of the word holds meanings of 'wise-man' and the verb 'to see,'" he writes. "To tell a story well is to see wisely, I say to myself."[1] I believe we desperately need wiser ways of seeing—and to that end, we need better stories.

No matter how much some of us might wish it, the people who don't vote like us or think like us aren't actually going anywhere. Clinton supporters didn't move to Canada after Trump's victory, and Trump supporters won't emigrate when he's out of office. Likewise, all those who voted against Brexit didn't exit Britain and Northern Ireland after the 2016 vote. For better or worse, we're all stuck here together. We should abandon our fantasies that one day when all is right with the world, we will no longer have to tolerate neighbors we find incomprehensible. We'll always live together.

We are wise to consider carefully how we might learn to live together well with those we find difficult. It's no great feat to enjoy living next to people you enjoy. That doesn't make for peace. What makes for peace is the capacity to live with difference in such a way that bears fruit rather than arms. Difference and disagreement are guaranteed for human relationships. More often than not, it's how we *deal with* difference,

1. Pádraig Ó Tuama, *In the Shelter: Finding a Home in the World* (London: Hodder and Stoughton, 2015), 106.

rather than *being* different, that determines our potential to be peaceable.

There's an old Irish saying: "Ar scáth a chéile a mhaireas na daoine." Pádraig, the person I just mentioned, says one could translate it as "It is in the shelter of each other that the people live." Another way is "It is in the shadow of each other that the people live." There's wisdom in those twists, not the least of which being that they tell us we can choose how we live together. Will we give shelter and welcome to each other, or will we let our shadows blot each other out? The stories we tell are part of how we make that choice.

The stories we tell either help us or harm us. No narrative is neutral. The ones that help are usually ones that tell bold truths about our world, even painful ones, because we always need to face the truth with courage if we're to heal and grow. The ones that hurt are usually ones that distort truths—maybe to protect power, or dehumanize, or tempt us to weaponize our fear. We humans tend to do our worst when we're afraid. Fear leads to hatred and hatred leads to violence and violence leads to fear, which leads to hatred, which leads to violence. If we don't address this deadly cycle, it can loop forever.

I've spent too much time in prisons and places of violent conflict to believe much good comes from being formed by fear. Stories of fear have their place—and this is an important thing to say. It would be untrue to say we should never be afraid. Fear is necessary. We need it to stay alive. And still, fear must be fruitful. When it's not, when it sees difference as dangerous, fear makes us into creatures of vitriol and violence. We all know this. When we're fueled by fear, we become paralyzed—or worse, *mobilized* in missions to eliminate whatever we're afraid of. With too many fear-forming stories, we may forget how to live with hope. And when hope dies, we all do.

The stories that might save us from this are stories that open us toward a fuller embrace of the world. These stories must, therefore, tell the truth. And part of the truth is that the world is full of violence, bereavements, and terrors that will terrorize even our dreams. This book will contain some of these stories because sometimes we need to hear them. Sometimes we can cushion ourselves in complacency and hide from the hardness of a world so many can't hide from. Sometimes we make ourselves believe—or simply choose to believe—stories that tame truths we might find inconvenient, or perhaps even detrimental, to what we consider fundamental. We stack simple stories onto the fault lines of our frail beliefs and sweep away stories that could challenge those beliefs. Because stories that tell counter-truths might shake our whole world. But sometimes we actually need our world to be shaken up. It can be part of what saves us.

And yet the agony of the world isn't the truth of the world; it's only part of the truth. Another part of the truth is that the world is full of beauty, friendship, and healing. The earth is populated with powerful stories of ordinary people doing extraordinary things, of inconceivable reconciliation, of faith and hope and love. Yet for some reason, we seem uninterested in these stories or are unwilling or unable to give them a platform. It seems that horror sells better than hope.

We have to do better. The stories we tell inform the breadth of our imaginations. Stories can help foster creative and prophetic imaginations; they help us find order and meaning within chaos, help us get our bearings when we feel lost. And stories can also foster bigotry, prejudice, and narrow-mindedness when told without wisdom.

Part of telling stories wisely is knowing one story cannot tell it all. I'm reminded often of prolific novelist Chimamanda

Ngozi Adichie's charge to resist "single stories": those stories that strip complexity from people and reduce them to narratives without nuance.[2] One of the first casualties in any conflict is nuance, and it's a slippery slope from there to rock bottom—where we usually take those rocks and launch them at each other. Single stories lure us toward the kind of thinking that leads to funerals. At best, they bore us; at worst, they bereave us. Single stories are a type of violence because they are a type of dehumanization.

Wise stories, however, are those that know that someone else might tell it differently. Wise stories know there is never one villain and never one hero. Wise stories know that sometimes, maybe even most times, people can be both. Wise stories know that if you describe characters as demonic, listeners will likely long for their destruction rather than redemption. Wise stories know that the wisest stories are not told by people in power.

Wise stories are ones that help us face the truth around us and name it for what it is. Throughout Pádraig Ó Tuama's book *In the Shelter*, he offers the simple tool of naming the truths around us and saying hello to them. Rather than pushing them away or pretending they aren't there or have no power, he encourages us to acknowledge them. Greet them. Say hello. See what we might learn from the situations and the strangers we did not choose—or at least did not know to name. I use this all the time now in my life as a way of acknowledging often unacknowledged truths, as a way of becoming familiar and maybe even friendly with what can be frightening. Because sometimes, simply saying hello might be part of what helps us.

---

2. Chimamanda Ngozi Adichie, "The Danger of a Single Story," filmed July 2009 in Oxford, UK, TED video, 18:43, https://www.ted.com/talks/chimamanda_adichie_the_danger_of_a_single_story/up-next.

MUCH OF WHAT PASSES for public storytelling today comes to us as "the news." And the news tends to be filled with stories of violence and division—and not in ways that teach us how to bridge these divides. We need to tell better stories than ones with violent beginnings, middles, and endings. I embarked on this story-gathering project because I wanted to help stretch my own imagination to be more generous and creative by meeting stories of people doing what so often seems impossible: choosing hope in the midst of despair.

In this book, I want to tell you these kinds of stories. I want to introduce you to incredible people from Palestine and Israel, Northern Ireland, and South Africa, people who have grown up and grown old in places of violent conflict and deep division. The people I've met during my travels in these countries are fully grounded in the pain *and* possibility of life. They know that no good comes from doing unto others the nightmares done unto us. They live with the kinds of stories that can wreck people, and they know that stories like that possess us—either devouring us like demons or enlivening us like water. They want new life to come from their loss. They seek peace out of pain.

In the biblical stories told in the book of Acts, there's a man named Saul who led persecutions of a new group of people who came to be known as Christians. He lived in fear of them, and they lived in fear of him. The writer of Acts tells us that one day, while traveling from Jerusalem to Damascus, Saul was blinded by a bright light and was confronted by the spirit of Jesus. Saul's whole world changed. For a few days, he lived in darkness. Then a man called Ananias came to him, placed hands on him, and what was blinding Saul left his eyes, and his sight returned. More than that, though, he could *see*, truly see—in ways he hadn't before.

Like Saul after the light, or the man from Bethsaida, many of us have been blind. We've been unable or unwilling to see the truth of our divisions. But the scales are falling from our eyes now. We're beginning to look with "eyes wide open," though our vision may still be blurred. We need wise others to meet us in our darkness and put hands on us so that we might finally see—wisely, with story.

The people and stories in this book can help us. They can show us not just *where* to look but *how* to look. They can orient us toward hope, and Lord knows we need it. In these pages, we hear from a peacebuilder about the dangers of dialogue that doesn't lead to freedom. We hear from a community center director on what to do when trauma is stuff of routine rather than stuff of memory. A former soldier teaches us to name what is wounded rather than ignore the pain, and a mother who lost her son shows us how to refuse vengeance. We meet a lover of Shakespeare who created a haven of beauty for those on the margins, and we encounter people who craft way stations of refuge for those in need of shelter. We hear how a woman made space in her life for the man who murdered her father. From a youth worker, we learn that reconciliation may mean little if it doesn't address the surrounding systems of inequality. From a community theater director, we hear of life under oppression and the journey to let go of the hatred that plagues like poison. And from two bereaved fathers, we are invited to imagine how we might meet devastating loss with grief and action.

Theirs are stories that might save us. Save us from believing that violence must be met with violence. Save us from believing that our belonging will be complete only when we take away someone else's. Save us from the prejudice that makes us predators. Save us from the myth of single stories. Save us from thinking that more guns, more walls, more armies can save us. They are stories that might save us from our fear.

These stories can help save us because they aren't stories of extraordinary people; they're stories of ordinary people who found themselves in extraordinary circumstances and simply did what they thought was right. They're people like us. Made of the same stuff. It would be too easy to dismiss these stories as the stuff of saints. Don't. The people I met have discovered a wisdom that tells them the world doesn't need another story of revenge or retribution. It needs a different story, one of reconciliation and hope. And if the world needs that from them, it needs it from all of us.

1

DIALOGUE IS NOT THE GOAL

I'm journaling in the garden at the Austrian Hospice in Jerusalem when I receive the email. This is one of my favorite spots in the Old City, just a couple of hundred yards down from Damascus Gate. I sip my frozen coffee—my fifth in two days, to be honest. The Austrian Hospice has the best I've ever tasted. The generous application of whipped cream may play a role in that.

The garden here is a green oasis in the middle of this ancient stone-walled city. Earlier today, I walked through storied streets where millions before me have walked, for hundreds of years. I have visited few places in the world where I feel more connected to the long thread of history than here in the Old City. So many stories converge and diverge. People have journeyed to this place for countless reasons: love, war, greed, faith, certainty, power, wondering, wandering, tradition, longing, escape, belonging. They meet here in this city for moments, then continue on. All these lives, these journeys, move and change, and this city with them. It's been here thousands of years, yet it constantly evolves.

The ding of my inbox brings me back to the garden. The email isn't long. In fact, I can read the whole thing in the preview text of the message. I wrote to a Palestinian professor a couple of weeks ago when I was home in Nashville. She didn't get back to me right away, but now she wastes no time getting to the point. My request was simple: I'd like to visit her university in the West Bank to speak with her and some of her students about their thoughts on reconciliation efforts between Israelis and Palestinians.

I glance at the preview text and open the message to be sure there's not more written. There's not. Though only sixteen words, her message contains a multitude of stories and frustrations and traumas and longings.

She's written, "This is an inappropriate conversation. We are being occupied. We should talk about justice not reconciliation."

THE EMAIL LANDS in my inbox on the anniversary of Michael Brown's murder by police officer Darren Wilson in Ferguson, Missouri. When Michael Brown was killed, I was on a retreat in Kentucky. The sound of a gunshot two states away was fueling a national movement that would change America. I came home to news reports of "angry protestors" and black people "rioting." People of color in Ferguson were rising up and taking the streets. They were calling for an end to the police violence that kills unarmed teenagers. They were calling for accountability for the officer who shot Mike Brown. They wanted the world to hear that black lives *matter*. In short, they wanted justice.

Ten months later, another horrific shooting happened. Self-proclaimed white supremacist Dylann Roof walked into Emanuel African Methodist Episcopal Church in Charleston, South Carolina, and started shooting. He murdered nine church members that day, all of whom were black: Sharonda Coleman-Singleton, Cynthia Graham Hurd, Susie Jackson, Ethel Lee Lance, DePayne Middleton-Doctor, Clementa C. Pinckney, Tywanza Sanders, Daniel Simmons Sr., and Myra Thompson. Only a few days after this, some of the family members of those Roof had killed faced him in court. And much to the surprise of the nation, some of those bereaved people forgave Roof. The news coverage about this response to white violence against black people was quite different. I remember words like *heroic* and *incredible* appearing in headlines.

This differing language awakened me. In both cases, an armed white person killed unarmed black people. In one case, bereaved and aggrieved people took to the streets demanding accountability and justice. In the other, bereaved and aggrieved people took the stand to extend forgiveness. And mainstream news—which in many ways is a manifestation of the white culture that dominates America—clearly preferred one response over the other.

This was my late arrival to a realization that many people, particularly marginalized and oppressed ones, have known for a long time: People in power prefer a victim calling for forgiveness and reconciliation to one calling for vindication. Forgiveness and reconciliation, it seems, suggest that the status quo may well endure; vindication suggests a reckoning is near. And reckonings rarely go well for those invested in nothing changing.

One thing this truth tells me is that we have developed quite destructive understandings of concepts like forgiveness and reconciliation. To hear the word *reconciliation* and not imagine a radical shift in unjust power structures is to me to see reconciliation as morally bankrupt, which I don't believe it is. This usually happens because language of reconciliation has been used as a tool to perpetuate people's burdened existence, or because keeping reconciliation morally bankrupt and boring props power up a while longer. In such cases, reconciliation is no friend to people on the underside of power. But those with the upper hand cozy up nicely to reconciliation, as it's one of the names given to the type of experiences that allow people to say, "How can I be racist? I have a black friend."

It's no surprise, then, that calls for justice energize people needing to level power, all while it makes the powerful batten down the hatches. Justice means things need to change. Reconciliation, at least the way the word is often used, means maybe everything can stay the same, as long as we're friendly. Most people on top don't want to be brought low. Why would they? And most people who are held down want the boot off their neck. Why wouldn't they?

The professor's email is timely and unsurprising. I read it again. "This is an inappropriate conversation. We are being occupied. We should talk about justice not reconciliation." While I'm saddened that the word *reconciliation* has been wielded in such a way as to seem dangerous to her, I understand her response. I have spent enough time in the West Bank to not be surprised by her refusal to talk about this subject. Honestly, though, it's this relationship of justice and reconciliation that I want to discuss. I want to dig deep into the effects that manipulative peace talks have had on the Palestinian posture toward notions of reconciliation. I am disappointed we won't get to talk, but I'm not going to try to reassure her and convince her. I'm going to let it go. Too many Palestinians

I know have been wounded by poison-pill notions of reconciliation. She has no reason to trust me. I suspect that to her I'm just another American stranger whose tax dollars fund her oppression. I probably would have denied me too.

I'M IN BETHLEHEM NOW. It's the morning of my first scheduled interview. I tell the Palestinian friends I'm staying with that I'm meeting Ali Abu Awwad. They know his name. His family is famous, and he himself has gained recognition as a Palestinian peacebuilder and advocate of nonviolence. I first encountered Ali through the documentary *Encounter Point.* That film was made in 2005, though, and I'm curious to see how his thoughts and work have changed.

I tell my friends I'm meeting Ali on his family land. His father bought the land as a legacy for his children in the 1970s after the trauma of 1948[1] displaced the family from Al-Qubeiba in Israel, leading to a series of exiles and border crossings, before returning to the West Bank to build a home in the nearby town of Beit Ummar. This family land lies along the highway near the Gush Etzion settlement junction on the road to Hebron. Settlements are Israeli towns built inside the Palestinian territories. International law considers the settlements illegal. Palestinians consider them colonies, one of the more permanent expressions of Israel's attempts to colonize Palestine. I agree. Whether you support settlement expansion

---

1. In November 1947, the United Nations partitioned Palestine into a Jewish state and an Arab one, which the Jews accepted and the Arab Palestinians did not. In the early months of 1948, Jewish paramilitaries, which would soon become the Israeli army, began removing thousands of Palestinians from their homes in certain border areas and around Jerusalem. On May 14, Israel announced its independence, and the next day, armies from surrounding Arab nations invaded, sparking a war with Israel. From the beginning of 1948 until the eventual ceasefires of 1949, over 750,000 Palestinians had been displaced. For Palestinians, this is called the *Nakba*, the Catastrophe.

or not, it is true that many, if not most, Palestinians consider settlements to be one of the largest obstacles to peace.

Ali has built a small shelter on his family's land, with a dream of creating a Palestinian nonviolence center. This place is also the site of the very thing I want to talk to him about: dialogues he hosts with the Israeli settlers nearby. When I tell my friends about this dialogue project—called Roots—they laugh out loud. I suspect a lot of Palestinians would have the same reaction. Some would see talking with settlers—who in many respects are the most extreme of the Israeli population—as a waste of time; others would see it as traitorous. In 2012, I spent a few months in Hebron with Christian Peacemaker Teams, a multifaith network transforming violence and oppression through nonviolent partnerships with people directly affected by deadly conflict. While in Hebron, I was advised not to talk with Israeli soldiers for fear of appearing I was normalizing the occupation. Talking with settlers wasn't even a consideration.

"I know it sounds really extreme," I say to my friends. "That's why I'm curious. Ali's a dedicated peacebuilder. I respect and trust his wisdom in this work, and so I want to hear why he thinks meeting with settlers is the right approach." They ask me to report back, and I catch a taxi to the bus station.

I find a van—called a "service" around here—that's heading from Bethlehem toward Hebron. Gush Etzion is on the way. I take the middle seat in the middle row, between a young woman and a middle-aged man. The man has a friendly smile. On the way, we exchange few words, since we don't speak each other's languages. Mostly, we shake our heads at erratic drivers. As we near his stop, his hand, which has been resting on the seat top behind me, moves to my head and gives my hair a gentle tug. I look at him, surprised. He just nods and says, "*Ahlan wasahlan,* most welcome." When the van stops to let him out, he tugs my hair once more for good measure.

Midway through the drive, the passengers all start gathering the fares for the driver, as if on cue. The young Muslim Palestinian woman sitting on my left stops studying for her summer exams for a moment and reaches in her purse to retrieve money for the taxi. I search my wallet for some shekels. I have no idea how much this costs, and the woman to my left can obviously tell. She holds up all the fingers on her right hand and says in lovely English, "It's five shekels." I smile, thank her, and look in my wallet. All I have is a hundred-shekel bill.

"No change?" she asks, seeing me hold up this unhelpfully large bill.

"Unfortunately not," I say, embarrassed. I ask her if the driver would take the hundred.

"How far are you going?" she asks. I don't know the name of Ali's land. The only name I know is that of the settlement bloc that's risen nearby. I don't want to tell her that I'm going to Gush Etzion, though. I'm not sure I can explain the nuances of why I'm getting off there.

I do not want this kind Palestinian woman to think I'm in support of settler colonization of her land. I'm not. In fact, I've dodged Israeli military gunfire marching in solidarity with her people's struggle for freedom. It feels important to me that she know I'm not another uncritical, uninformed American. But then I decide none of that is her problem. She asked me where I was going, so I tell her and brace myself for a justified look of disdain.

"The settlement?" she clarifies.

"Yes, *mustawtana,*" I say.

She smiles. I didn't expect that. "Here," she says, producing another five-shekel coin, "I will pay for yours." I definitely did not expect that. I protest—strongly—but to no avail. She waves me off, hands her coin to the driver, and returns to her studies.

I WALK DOWN A LONG DIRT ROAD to reach Ali's place. Per usual in Palestine, I'm offered coffee before I've really said hello. I take a seat in a yellow chair in the outdoor common space under a large awning made of tan tarp. Ali sits next to me. His brown watch matches his shoes, and his greenish-gray button-up is tucked into his blue jeans. His black hair is still as curly as it was in the videos I've seen of him, and his face is weathered and kind.

Having watched *Encounter Point* many times, I know a bit of Ali's story. I know his brother was shot dead by a soldier at a checkpoint. I know Ali joined the Parents Circle-Families Forum, an organization of bereaved Israelis and Palestinians using their shared suffering as a tool for reconciliation. I know Ali gained international notoriety for speaking out for nonviolence even in the wake of his brother's murder. I know some Palestinians find him inspirational because of this, and others find him problematic.

Sitting with him now, I feel his sincerity, as if he has woven it into a quilt and wrapped it around my shoulders. His wisdom and abilities are in high demand, and yet he is sitting with me, an American writer he's never heard of, and treating our conversation as if it's the only thing happening in the world. That type of presence is hard to come by.

Ali asks me about my project.

"I'm spending the next few months traveling around your country, Northern Ireland, and South Africa to meet with peacebuilders and listen to their stories and wisdom about the possibilities and problems of reconciliation."

"And what have you learned so far?" he asks.

Fair enough. If I'm going to ask him questions, it's only right he gets to put me on the spot too. I reflect on the email I received at the Austrian Hospice in Jerusalem and the thinking I've done since.

"I've learned that reconciliation efforts can be problematic if we aren't careful. There's something about the language of reconciliation that can seem friendlier to those in power and an enemy to those suffering, while language of justice may be the exact opposite. I've learned that if pursuits of reconciliation are not intimately tied up with works of justice, then so-called reconciliation may be unhelpful. In fact, it may actually be harmful."

Ali flashes a wide smile. "Bravo!" he says, nodding. "This is very important." And then he starts in, talking first about the reconciliation efforts he was once part of a decade before. "We used to meet—Israeli and Palestinian activists—we used to meet in five-star peace conferences where we hug each other and eat hummus and we feel good about ourselves. And we think we make peace by doing that. And this is nice. This is good, really. Knowing is very important. But what is next, in a practical way, that will serve people's life conditions? Peace is not to create another bubble. Peace is to bring all the values of legitimate rights into harmony with our daily movements.

"I don't want to hear a nice speech from Israelis. This is not my goal. *Dialogue* is not my goal. Dialogue is a tool, a carrier from one side's truth to a bigger truth that also includes the other side. But also, dialogue is not necessarily a place of comfort. Dialogue can be so tough sometimes, especially when it is between enemies, when they have no idea who the other side is. But at the same time, I believe that dialogue for two traumatized nations should be a secure place for arguments."

This is the second time in a week now that I've heard that sentiment: Dialogue isn't the goal. It's a method of achieving legitimate rights for all people, to improve people's life conditions. And if it's not the goal, then what's the point? I listen with full attention to Ali as he continues talking, telling me why he's in dialogue with the settlers surrounding his land.

"I will speak to anyone about my freedom," he says. "When I came here, I was not expecting Mandelas to come out from these settlements. I knew very well that I am dealing with the toughest community in Israel. And I know that my suffering didn't come from nice left Tel Avivis." He's talking about the political leanings of Israelis in Tel Aviv, the largest and most liberal city in Israel.[2] "My suffering comes from these settlements," he says pointing to the area surrounding us. "The conflict will never change as long as we think we only need to see the humanity of each other's identity. This must happen, yes. But we must also change the *behavior*. It is not the *identity* of Israelis, of these settlers, that is occupying my country; it is their *behavior*."

Ali says he wants the settlers to know him. He wants to open a window to their community, even a small one, so they might see the consequences of their behavior. The impact of their fear. He hopes to call them away from that fear.

"Don't use that fear," he says. "Don't let it blind you. Because the minute that you do that, you are not victimizing just me or my people; you are victimizing yourself. And this fear of the Jewish nation has become an identity, a bubble

---

2. If you google this claim—that Tel Aviv is the largest city in Israel—you will likely find sources that list Jerusalem as the largest city. The list usually goes: Jerusalem, Tel Aviv, West Jerusalem, and so on. This means that the Jerusalem listed first includes East Jerusalem, the part of the city claimed by Palestine as its capital. To do that is to normalize Israel's occupation of that part of the city, to ignore the contested nature of it, and to erase the Palestinian claim of East Jerusalem as its capital. I thus list Tel Aviv as the largest city.

around Israeli politics. And whether we like it or not as Palestinians, that fear is our biggest enemy. Because of that fear, we've become occupied."

A group arrives. It seems Ali was scheduled to address this group at the same time as our conversation. Works for me. I'll listen to his talk and then follow up after.

He begins with an overview of his story. "I was born in 1972 to a refugee family from 1948." When he says 1948, he's using shorthand to reference what Palestinians call the Nakba. In Arabic, it means "catastrophe," and it refers to the displacement of 750,000 Palestinians in the months surrounding the establishment of the state of Israel in May 1948. Ali's family was one of those displaced. He was born a refugee in the West Bank, separated from the land his family had called home for generations.

Ali tells us he was born into a very political family. His mother was one of the popular leaders of the Palestinian liberation movement and was close to the infamous Yasser Arafat. He says of that time, "We drink politics, we eat politics, we breathe politics under this title of resistance. We are the heroes who are resisting the occupier." Eventually, his home came under fire from the Israeli military. Arrests. Beatings. He saw his family humiliated and brutalized by Israeli soldiers for their resistance. Ali says, "Sometimes people ask me why Palestinians educate their kids to hate, which is the most—I'm sorry to say it—the most stupid question. Because if you live in such conditions, I'm not sure you need a specific curriculum for hate."

Ali tells us how, at seventeen, he became trained in the use of weapons and hurled stones at the Israeli military during the first intifada, the first national Palestinian uprising. It began at the end of 1987 and ended with the Oslo Peace Accords in

1993. Though he never used his weapons training, Ali and his mother were arrested and tortured numerous times during the intifada. One of Ali's tortures lasted one month and six days.

"And I promise you," he says, "at that time, I was dreaming, hoping that I would die any minute rather than face all of that. I was seventeen years old." A couple of little puppies run into the circle of chairs and begin playing at Ali's feet while he tells us about his torture. The Israeli interrogators wanted him to give up information on his mother. He refused, and Israel sentenced him to ten years in prison.

"I was totally broken," Ali says after a pause. "Because I had dreams. I wanted to travel. I wanted to study. And I had a crazy Palestinian dream to be a pilot. Because where to fly? I have no passport. Who would accept me at all? But you know," he says, smiling, "kids dream. And maybe that dream was just because I wanted to be higher than this environment that raised you to hate *yourself*, not just your enemy."

Despite the devastation of such a sentence at such a young age, Ali says prison was the first place he felt he had dignity. His fellow prisoners created an organized education system to keep their minds and resistance active. Incarcerated, he learned the principles and practice of nonviolence. Hunger strikes became a primary tool for getting the things they needed. Upon his release after the Oslo Accords, Ali joined the security forces for the newly formed Palestinian Authority (PA). One of the PA's responsibilities was to prevent Palestinian violence against Israel, which was a complicated job for Ali.

"The PA's responsibility was to stop violent attacks," he says, "but we were also being challenged by the continuation of the military occupation on the ground. So we couldn't prove to the Palestinian nation that violence is illegitimate because we couldn't bring political rights to their lives. So

I became embarrassed and ashamed by peace. We signed a peace agreement, but it has become a piece of paper. Peace is not to sign a piece of paper; it's to bring what is on paper to the ground. To change life conditions, to bring independence, security for both sides."

I can see why Ali has become a leader. He's not building a peace brand that relies on inspirational, vague language about bridges and getting along and seeing the humanity in one another (all of which are important). He's talking about actual concrete improvements to the quality of one's life. If peacebuilding isn't dealing with that, then it's not building peace.

What he's talking about now is his *lived* experience with the kind of stuff I've only studied. In graduate school in Belfast, we discussed how pieces of paper don't make for peace. That's not to say peace accords are irrelevant. The language of those accords is essential in mapping the path forward. As Rabbi Abraham Joshua Heschel is often quoted as saying, "Words make worlds." But people on the ground then have to populate those worlds with the building blocks of peace. So I get what Ali is saying—a blueprint isn't a house, and a peace accord doesn't mean there's peace. It means there's an agreement to try to *build* peace. As peacebuilder John Paul Lederach says, what you really need is people for the *day after* the agreement.

Ali says that during the second intifada, which erupted in late 2000, he was shot in the knee and had to seek treatment in Saudi Arabia. This is the part of the story I'd heard before. Ali's mother went to be with him.

"After one month of being with my mother," Ali says, "I heard my older brother Yousef, thirty-one years old, was stopped at the entrance of my village Beit Ummar and very violently killed by an Israeli soldier. He had two kids, and he was the best human being I have ever met. Everyone loved that guy. He was unarmed and never engaged in any violent actions. There was an argument with a soldier that cost him his life. So what do you do after all that?"

I think of all the stories in the United States of black people shot dead by cops who decided that, like these soldiers, their guns were the quickest and safest way for them to end the interaction. And honestly, I have no idea what you do after all that.

"Before I was born, after I was born, until now," Ali continues, "a story of suffering. The normal reaction is revenge. By revenge, you want to create a punishment. You think that revenge is to create justice. But what kind of punishment is just? The pain is so huge, the revenge must be more so. How many Israelis do I have to kill to bring him back? How many Israeli mothers must cry to experience this salty taste of my mother's tears? But if all Israel could disappear, my brother would still not come back. So what can justice be? Is it to punish the perpetrator? This won't be enough to heal that pain. My brother's life is more holy than anything. When God created all this, he made it for us to enjoy from it, not sacrifice from it. How do we create a normal act from an abnormal environment? So I was stuck—conflicted between my political mind that was convinced in prison about nonviolence, and between my bleeding heart."

I hear the sounds of a helicopter overhead and cars on the highway nearby as Ali recounts for us his entrance into the Parents Circle. An Israeli religious Jew, whose son had been captured and killed by Hamas, paid his condolences to Ali's family and invited them to join a group. This group comprised Israeli and Palestinian families who had been bereaved through the years of killing. This shared sense of loss is the common ground where they stand to see each other's equal humanity. Ali was shocked that such a group existed.

"Israelis don't seek for peace," he tells us, describing the narrative he'd developed at that time, after more than two decades of painful experience. "Even victims in Israel seek revenge. It was shocking that an Israeli was calling us, 'Come to our home.' Israelis never call to come to their home. They come and damage. They don't come as guests. And Israelis don't see us. They don't recognize our pain. They don't recognize our rights."

In 2001, when he met families involved in the Parents Circle, it was the first time Ali saw an Israeli not as *occupier*.

"I couldn't even in my imagination imagine that Jewish people have tears, or they have feelings regarding what they cause us," he says. "This is not the face that you see in checkpoint. These are not the same people. This is not the language or the behavior of the occupier anymore. Then I told myself if this group, who has paid the highest price in the conflict, are willing to act with us for a better future, everything is possible."

This possibility became his life. Ali dove into work with the Parents Circle. He traveled the world, attending conferences and summits, speaking to anyone and everyone who would listen. But eventually, he says, he realized he was living in a bubble. He was spending his time speaking with people who believed what he believed, who wanted what he wanted. People who were on his team, so to speak. All this was and is important. Building capacity among like-minded people is essential peace work. But still, Ali says, it wasn't the work he wanted to do anymore. He was done preaching to the choir. If peace was going to happen, for *real*, he needed to reach his *real* enemies: the settlers.

Here near Gush Etzion, Ali has helped begin an initiative called Roots. He creates a space where Israeli settlers and Palestinians can come together without needing any kind of permit to cross over borders or through checkpoints. Ali says it's about "transformation, nonviolence, and understanding."

"We don't speak about reconciliation ever," he says. "It's not there yet."

I feel such respect for Ali as he is speaking to us. Not only is he fighting an uphill battle with the settlers, but he is also risking the ire of his own community. Often when conversations about reconciliation come up, especially when these conversations assume the presence of dialogue between Palestinians and Israelis, many Palestinians recoil and condemn it as "normalization." In the nearly twenty years I've been traveling here, I've heard this word often. Tremendous power imbalances are at work through the occupation. Pushing for dialogue can come dangerously close to normalizing the disparate power realities on the ground, whether intentionally or not. For a Palestinian to show up and sit side by side with an Israeli can feel as if they are supposed to pretend all is equal. Their worth as people is equal, of course, but their lived experiences of justice and freedom are not. Ali's sitting with settlers will certainly spark anger in some of his compatriots.

But Ali tells us again that dialogue with settlers—or with anyone else, for that matter—is not his goal. "Part of the problem is dialogue has become a goal for many Israelis," he says. "Dialogue is not my goal. Dialogue is my carrier to freedom. So what are you expecting of me? To be a nice Palestinian that is always speaking about peace? I will not do that. I cannot do that."

The moment he says this, I know those words may be some of the most important I hear during my next three months of travel through divided societies. "Dialogue is not my goal.

Dialogue Is my carrier to freedom." In other words, dialogue as an end unto itself is an inappropriate conversation because it likely benefits only those in power.

I am thinking now of respectability politics, as it's called back home. Of how in the United States, white people like me tend to have all kinds of ways we want people of color to express their anger. The first is that we'd like them not to be angry. Frustrated, maybe; concerned, okay. But what we really want is for people of color to assume we're doing the best we can and (perhaps) to inform us *gently* of an occasional misstep so as to *encourage* us and not cause us feelings of guilt for the consequences of our whiteness. Given what Ali is saying, I'm assuming that this is true to some degree in Israel as well. "So what are you expecting of me?" Ali has just asked. "To be a nice Palestinian that is always speaking about peace?" I imagine that when Ali speaks about the injustices suffered by Palestinians because of the occupation, some Israelis listening may respond the way some—or most—white people back home do: "Enough talking about all the problems. Do you have a solution? If everything is so bad, what's your plan for fixing it? And if you don't have a plan, why haven't you left yet since life is so miserable for you?" It's hard to imagine solutions together, though, if you don't agree on the problems. It'd be like medical professionals trying to agree on treatment when they disagree on the diagnosis. The diagnosis matters. To act like it doesn't matter is to likely feel responsible, or at least fear you'll be *held* responsible, for the disease.

When the news media started covering Ferguson and Baltimore and all the other black intifadas at home, I do not know how many times I heard a good-hearted white person say something like, "Why can't we all just sit down and talk together? Why do they need to protest like this? Can't we all just dialogue together respectfully?" Ali has given me the language now to ask, "Dialogue to what end?" Because the dialogue can't be the goal. We've got to dream beyond that. Dialogue must always be a tool in service of liberation, of more justice and equity and human rights. If it's not, then it can become a means of maintaining oppression.

I return my focus to Ali. He's mentioning the national nonviolent movement he's spearheading called Taghyeer, which means "change" in Arabic. This nonviolence, he says, is about deepening trust within the Palestinian community, giving up acting as victims and taking responsibility for their fate, forcing themselves and the occupation they resist to encounter their humanity, and building up the power of Palestinians to work together for lasting change.[3] He's also talking about the complications of a one-state versus a two-state political resolution. He tells us that whatever path these two societies choose, there's a price to pay.

"The question is," Ali says, "are we able to accept the painful price of peace or the painful price of war? Because we are victims. The price of war is still more acceptable than the price of peace. And this competition of suffering between us and this competition of rightness keeps us dying. I promise you, Israel will not disappear. Palestine will not disappear. We are here. This is our destiny. Whether we are left wing, right wing, peacemakers, extremists—this is the reality today. So how will we be able to manage living here with values of dignity, freedom, peace, whatever, and stop this competition? It's by knowing and acting, without denying the other truth."

---

3. See more about Taghyeer at https://www.friendsoftaghyeer.org/. As of publication of this book, Ali's primary efforts are ensuring the growth of Taghyeer Movement among Palestinians in the West Bank, and developing Karama (Dignity)—the Palestinian Nonviolence Center—on his family's land. While supporting his legacy in Roots and its local efforts, Ali no longer represents or speaks for that initiative.

I glance at my phone to check the time. I need to leave soon if I'm going to make my next meeting. Almost as if he could sense this, Ali begins to wrap up.

"So peace, by the end of the day, is not just about partnership. It's about our choice as a Palestinian to adopt nonviolence to become an identity and carry us from suffering and injustice to freedom and dignity. This is what we believe. Even if we will not have Israeli followers, this is our choice. This is our strategy, and that's our belief."

AFTER THE CONVERSATION WRAPS UP, I gather my things and extend my hand to Ali in thanks.

"Was this helpful?" he asks me. "Did you hear what you hoped to hear?"

"More than you know," I assure him.

On the ride back to Bethlehem, I'm lost in thought. Driving through the heart of the West Bank, I look out the window. Israeli flags. Military towers. Barracks. Settlements. Soldiers. Ali's land is occupied. He has lived under the control of another government his entire life. And this has led him to know that dialogue and relationships matter because separateness can breed single stories. This life has also led him to know that dialogue and relationships only matter so much. If pursuits of dialogue and relationship with those on the other side are not actively leading toward a secure, peaceful, just, and equitable future for all involved, then they aren't worth having.

I'm grateful that Ali's story and the Palestinian professor's email marked the beginning of this journey. I wasn't expecting this.

2

WE HAVE NO PTSD

The night lights of Tel Aviv's coastline are striking. They're not unlike any other Western coastal city, yet I still feel mesmerized staring at them. My new friend Asher is next to me. He's an Israeli physician and the friend of a friend of my father's. We've been wandering through a south Tel Aviv festival for the last couple of hours, discussing everything from marriage to religion to war.

After a while, Asher suggests we stroll along the beach and up through Old Jaffa for a panorama of the coastline. He tells me stories of his soldiering in Gaza as we hike the hills, our sandaled feet blistering. Now we are standing on the cobblestone walkways of HaMidron Garden, looking at the shining city on the waterfront.

"So what's it like in the West Bank?" he asks.

"Have you never been there?" I say.

"Only as a soldier," he says.

I look out past the lit skyline of Tel Aviv, toward the dark-ened hills of the West Bank. "Palestine is beautiful," I say. "It's full of life and laughter. People are friendly, the food is delicious, the history is remarkable. There's so much creativity there, so much kindness, and hospitality. And there's also a lot of brokenness and despair. The people are weary of being occupied. They want freedom. The vast majority want peace. They want to live as neighbors, not as enemies."

Asher is listening intently to me. His gaze joins mine toward the distant hills.

"I wish we didn't have to occupy their land," he says after a few moments of silence. "I went to Hebron when I was in the army, and I saw the way we make them live. It's terrible. I know some people call it apartheid. And in some ways, I think they are right." I did not expect to hear him say that, and I try to mask my surprise. "But we have to do this," he continues. "We must control them. If we don't, they will attack us. This is exactly what happened in Gaza. We had our people there until 2005, and as soon as we pulled out, Hamas took over and began launching attacks against us. I hate that this is the reality"—he shakes his head, searching the night sky as if for answers—"but I fear they will kill us if we don't control them. It's the cost of security."

I consider his face for a few moments, wondering what to say. I don't believe that what he says is true, but I take his fear seriously. The violence of this hundred-year-old conflict has decimated trust between the people here, at least for now. Without trust, or the willingness to risk for trust, there can be no peace. Given some of the history here and especially how the story of the history is told, I have no trouble understanding why Asher believes what he believes.

"This is why peace in long-standing conflicts is so elusive," I say to him. "Both sides have so many stories—both true and exaggerated—about why the other can't be trusted. Few are willing to risk setting the gun down to talk because you can't be absolutely certain the other person won't shoot you once you do. And then you get into fierce debates about who started it all, and eventually, all the arguments over who fired the first shot become less relevant. There are too many murders on both sides. And in the end, bereavement is bereavement, whether your loved one is dead from the first shot or the shot that was fired back."

He nods and says, "Some of my friends were killed while we were serving in Gaza."

"I am very sorry to hear that," I say. We stand in silence for a bit. My eyes move back and forth from the harbor to the city lights to the dark expanse of the Mediterranean Sea. Asher fixes his eyes on the water.

"You know," he says, "recently I was thinking to myself, 'What is the one thing I cannot live without?' And I realized that the only thing I could never live without is the sea. For me, the sea is freedom. It's the symbol of ultimate freedom. The sea contains beauty and endless possibilities. When I look out at the horizon of the sea, it appears limitless. This is freedom to me." Asher turns toward me. "Really, Michael, if you take the sea away from me, I'd die."

I rotate my body slightly away from the water and point my finger northeast toward the West Bank. "Over there is Nablus. I was there not too long ago with my dad, and we met with some medical students who took us out on a roof of a building on one of the tallest hills. It was a clear day, and they told us to look out west past the distant hills to the blue on the horizon. I could see the slightest sparkle along the blue. They said it was the Mediterranean Sea. They said that on certain days from certain hills, they could see the sea. And yet, among these medical students who have lived their entire lives seeing the sea from their native hills, not one had ever been allowed to visit it. Imagine that. This sea that means freedom, the one thing you can't live without—imagine seeing it all your life but never being permitted to go."

The way he's looking at me now, I wonder if he might cry. His eyes are sad and serious. "That is torture," he says, shaking his head. "I cannot imagine." His focus returns to the waves. "It's terrible. It's not right."

I smile at Asher's courage to say that. In conflict, it's not easy to imagine the other's life could be yours. Empathy can be the beginning of big changes. As we start the walk back through the city to my hostel, Asher says, "If you're still in Tel Aviv tomorrow night, come and have dinner with my family. My wife and parents would love to meet you."

"I'd be delighted," I say, grateful for a new friend.

THE WI'AM Palestinian Conflict Transformation Center is not hard to find. The sign out front certainly helps, but even without it, the location is easy enough. It's nestled between two Bethlehem landmarks: the expansive Jacir Intercontinental Hotel and Israel's separation wall. A graffiti-covered sniper tower sits so close I could pelt it with a rock. Standing here at the turquoise gate, I scan the wall, twice the height of the one that was in Berlin. Just over its razor wire, I can see an Israeli settlement. On this side of the wall, a minaret rises from the Aida refugee camp down the hill. This is quite the location for a center dedicated to transforming conflict. I push open the gate and descend the stone steps.

A man named Usama greets me, hospitality emanating from him like steam. He invites me to sit, and prepares tea while the center director, Dr. Zoughbi Zoughbi, finishes a phone call. Usama begins telling me of the beautiful work happening at Wi'am, how they use storytelling, gardening, mediation training, play, lectures, tours, dialogue, and much more to "keep the hope alive," especially for the young people in community.

"We promote the traditional Palestinian method of *sulha*," Usama says to me, "seeking to dismantle the occupation and secure freedom through nonviolence." He pours the amber tea into a small glass. "What you take for granted in America, we die for here," he says.

Dr. Zoughbi walks in, smiling through thin-rimmed glasses and his salt-and-pepper goatee. He leads me to his desk. "Welcome to Palestine," he says. I thank him, and ask if he can tell me about this remarkably situated community center, designed to help people resolve conflict in a nonviolent way. He tells me he founded the center in 1994 to respond to the needs of his local community. "We decide to work on community building through civil society programs for children, youth, women, men through the conflict resolution that result in our daily life, and also through the act of nonviolent protest that we take against the occupation. And of course through advocacy, we try to empower the work of our people to self-determination and statehood."

I'm encouraged hearing him talk of nonviolence. Ali spoke of it too. Back home in Nashville, and in plenty of other places in the United States, people often assume that Palestinians are a violent people. Obsessed with terrorism. Bent on destroying Israel and America. Eager to blow up anything and anyone Western.

One time, in a Nashville church, I told some of my stories from working with Christian Peacemaker Teams in Hebron. I finished the talk and opened the floor for questions. A woman near the back raised her hand and said, "Could you tell us what it was like to be surrounded by Arabs who wanted to kill you?" This was revealing on two fronts. First, I had not referred to *Arabs*; instead, I had told stories of my interactions with *Palestinians*. Refusing to call the people of Palestine *Palestinians* is a tool for delegitimizing their claim to the land. And second, all the violence I had spoken of in the stories came at the hands of Israeli soldiers. That's not to say that Palestinians have never been violent; of course they have. But the violence in my experiences came from Israel Defense Forces (IDF) soldiers. This person could simply not believe that I lived in the West Bank for three months and faced no threat from the millions of Palestinians around me.

Dr. Zoughbi adjusts some papers on his desk as he tells me that through nonviolence Wi'am strives "to empower the weak and to bring the strong to their senses." I love that idea of bringing the strong to their senses. It's insightful. There's certainly a sense in which militarily controlling an entire people has moved beyond a creative imagination for sensible living. Dr. Zoughbi says he wants to help "save the soul of Israel" by liberating it through liberating his own people. Free the oppressed and you might free the oppressor too.

"We invite people from around the world to come, see, observe, learn, and act," he says. "Because we don't want you to be pro-Palestinian. We want you to be pro-justice: justice that helps us live to celebrate life and not death. Instead of pointing the finger at others to blame, we entice collective responsibility, because collective responsibility is the cure for all."

Just outside the door of this center is Israel's wall. Scattered along the base, Palestinian artists have stamped MADE IN THE USA to remind Americans of how U.S. tax dollars are at work in their homeland. Israel is the highest recipient of U.S. foreign aid, and millions of those dollars were used to build this barrier. Seeing the graffiti reminds me that, as Rabbi Heschel said, "some are guilty, and all are responsible."

"This is very important," Dr. Zoughbi tells me. "We don't want to inherit the guilt in others, because it will paralyze us. We don't want to dwell on victimhood, because it is suicidal. We don't want to blame others, because it is toxic. *All together*, we'll be able to end the occupation. We believe in nonviolence as a way to struggle against the occupation. We believe that we are not against Jews; we are against the occupation. We would like to coexist, whether in two states or one state."

Then Dr. Zoughbi talks to me about the center's work with the traumatized youth of their community. Over the years here, I've become educated about the traumas facing the young people. Arrests. Detentions. Beatings. Bullets. Tear gas. Sound bombs. Handcuffs. Checkpoints. Frisking. Armed soldiers. Dead friends. Disappeared parents. Nighttime home invasions. Controlled movement. Family separation. Inconsistent access to education because of military closures. And forced powerlessness, often through personal humiliation or watching the humiliation of parents. Humiliation like strip searches. Multiple trips through metal detectors. Being detained randomly without explanation. Being forced to lie facedown in the dirt on command. Arbitrary denials of entry to Israel despite having written permission. Having to do literally anything a soldier says. And on and on and on.

Dr. Zoughbi says that Wi'am's programs must face these traumas, and thus, they can't focus on trauma healing.

"You don't try to do trauma healing?" I ask. Trauma healing—the process of recovering and moving on from the control that traumatic experiences have on a person—gets a lot of attention in conflict transformation and social justice circles these days, and I'm surprised Wi'am doesn't do it.

"No, because we don't have the post-traumatic stress disorder. It's *ongoing* trauma, layer after layer. There's no way that it is *post*. It's real. And you can see the trauma in all, kids and adults. And you can see it in bed-wetting for kids, nightmares, involuntary urination, conflicts at home. So you need trauma coping."

For some reason, this takes a minute to sink in. They have no PTSD. Not because there's no trauma, but because there's never *not* trauma. It happens all the time, every day. I think of communities of color back home. I suspect many would say the same thing Dr. Zoughbi said—whether because of encounters with law enforcement, or living in a society determined to inject its racism any place it can, or having to cope with the constant threat of deportation.

A week or so before I left Nashville for Tel Aviv, a police officer pulled me over. I texted the friend I was en route to see, "Just got pulled over. Be a few minutes late." This experience with police is a world apart from April's, a young black woman who told me she keeps her insurance and license clipped to her driver side visor so she never has to reach her hands below an officer's eyesight when pulled over. She told me how her whole body tightens near the point of panic when she sees flashing blue lights in her rearview mirror. She told me how her brother had just bought a new car nine months earlier from the money he saved from his great new job working for a healthcare corporation. She told me cops had already pulled him over seventeen times. Seventeen. Apparently, how it is that a young black man might be able to drive a yellow convertible in certain Nashville neighborhoods is worthy of police investigation.

I'm also thinking of a time in Hebron in January 2012 when I met a boy, around sixteen years old, whose head was wrapped in bandages. That morning, his older brother, who everyone knew lived with developmental disabilities, was beaten by Israeli soldiers while passing through a checkpoint to refill the gas canister for their home. The soldiers came to the family's house that night, grabbed the boy I met, and beat his head with their rifle butts until his skull cracked.[1] It was the second time that month he'd been abused by the military. This is the kind of trauma children must cope with.

"For kids," Dr. Zoughbi says, bringing my attention back, "we try to help them with art, through storytelling, through theater, through dancing, through art therapy, through playing together. We really work hard to provide kids with safe environment. We don't want to have our youth monopolized by pain or compete for victimhood. We would like our youth to celebrate life, and be assertive but not aggressive. And through our youth exchange and programs for youth, we are able to address many of the issues.

"You know, one-third of the male population has been in jail. Twenty thousand women in our population have been in jail. So the whole society has been in jail. We live in a big prison, and we have small prisons. If Martin Luther King was alive, he would write a letter from Bethlehem jail, from Jericho jail, from Hebron jail. So this is the situation of our youth, and 70 percent of our population is under the age of thirty. You know, women suffer a lot from patriarchal society,

---

1. For more of this story, see Michael T. McRay, *Letters from "Apartheid Street": A Christian Peacemaker in Occupied Palestine* (Eugene, OR: Cascade Books, 2013), 23–24.

from displaced anger from the male in the society, and from the occupation, of course. And we try to empower them for gender justice."

He hesitates. Not as if he's trying to decide what to say next; more as if he wishes he didn't have to say it. "It is not easy to live here," he says, lifting his brow. Then he nods. "But we have the resilience, the steadfastness, and the perseverance."

His available time is up. He had generously agreed to meet with me between other commitments today, and now he's running late for what's next.

"Thank you so much for speaking with me," I say. His grip, like his conviction, is firm as we shake hands. "You are most welcome to Palestine," he says with a warm smile. I lift my backpack off the chair next to me, thank Usama for his hospitality, and leave the way I entered.

My walk back to the checkpoint is quite simple if I follow the wall. It's such a prodigious eyesore, snaking its way through town, and throughout the rest of the West Bank. Israel says this wall is for security. Given that it sprang up during the height of the suicide bombing campaign of the second intifada, there's a case to be made for a wall as a necessary security measure. The problem is that 85 percent of this barrier is on Palestinian land, inside the West Bank. It doesn't run along the Green Line— the armistice line of 1949—which is the only internationally recognized border between Israel and Palestine. This would be like building a wall along the U.S.-Mexico border to reduce so-called illegal immigration but constructing it in and around Juarez, Tijuana, Reynosa, Monterrey, and even Chihuahua. You might ask yourself whether the wall is to keep out immigrants from Central and South America, or whether preventing illegal immigration has become a front for seizing Mexican land.

That's what I think of every time I walk beneath this wall Dividing lands, dividing families, dividing peoples. The illusion of safety for those inside and the imprinting of the reality of confinement for another. Walls like these often rise in response to fear. When I lived in Belfast for grad school, I encountered what are called the "peace walls," mostly erected after the signing of the Good Friday Agreement in 1998, which ended the Troubles. In that part of the world, there's a saying: "Whatever you say, say nothing." Because you don't know whom to trust. People need to feel safe, and we fear whatever threatens our safety. So we say to our leaders, "Build us walls. Keep us safe from one another."

But I think walls become self-fulfilling prophecies. We put up walls because we fear an "other." Then years go by, and new generations rise in the shadow of these barriers. Even if any credible threat on the other side is long gone, the walls can't come down, because the nature of their existence has taught those around them that something beyond the wall should indeed be feared. Walls like the one looming above me now create a need to exist by simply existing. They end up perpetuating fear, and with fear, conflict.

I round the bend, passing a gas station first and then the new boutique Walled Off Hotel, established by the mysterious renowned artist Banksy, whose recognizable graffiti style decorates walls around the West Bank. Keeping the wall to my left, I stay on the edge of the road, avoiding traffic, reading as much of the new graffiti as I can, and scanning the text and colors for old favorites. I love the one of a weeping Lady Liberty cradling Handala, a cartoon drawing of a refugee child that has become a symbol of Palestinian struggle for justice. And the one that reads, "I can't believe I'm still protesting this s---."[2] In purple text, I see "Justice without love is nothing." There are road signs plastered on the wall that read "Wall Street" and "Apartheid Avenue." In giant green and gray and yellow lettering, Miley Cyrus lyrics make an appearance: "I came in like a wrecking ball!" And Handala stands with his hands behind his back, peering through a crack in the wall, gazing upon unreachable blue waters.

I exit a narrow road onto a wider one. The checkpoint is visible now, with its long, barred, cage-like passageway leading up a small incline along the wall. I've never had much trouble here. My blue U.S. passport tends to sail me through.

Crossing through a turnstile and under the wall, I cross a bit of open pavement and enter the next section of the checkpoint, zigzagging down a walkway that leads to metal detectors and the security check. I have no problem, despite all the metal I'm carrying. The Palestinians next to me who are trying to cross are made to remove every ounce of metal on their person. It takes them at least twice as long. An old man next to me, wearing a traditional Arabic *thawb* and *keffiyeh* headdress, is forbidden to pass until he removes his headdress, ensuring he's without explosives. He shakes his head as he lifts the red-checkered covering from his hair.

As I near the ID check, which is the final station, all I can hear is shouting. A soldier examines the green Palestinian IDs and permission papers of the people in front of me, allowing some through and turning others away. A child next to me is weeping as he learns he won't be allowed to go to Jerusalem. Each Palestinian in line places their fingers on a scanner. The soldier searches for their fingerprints in his computer. Then he waves some forward and sends some back, splitting up a

---

2. Editorial guidelines at Herald Press restrict the use of profanity in its publications.

family. The parents and the young soldier on the other side of the glass exchange heated words.

I hold up my passport. He glances at it and waves me through. On the checkpoint wall in front of me as I exit are a series of posters. One says, "Israel, The Roots of Peace." Another says, "Tel Aviv-Jaffa, for the time of your life!" And still another, "Welcome to Israel, It's Vacation All Year Round!" I step out in the sun to board Bus 24, leaving the sound of two sobbing children behind me.

3

SOMETHING IS WOUNDED

From his Facebook profile picture, the former Israeli soldier looks about my age. I am to meet him in West Jerusalem in half an hour, so I leave the Old City through Jaffa Gate and descend into the outdoor Mamilla Mall. I stop at an intersection to wait for cars to pass. Once clear, I cross the road despite the red pedestrian light. No one here actually obeys traffic laws.

Google Maps said it would take about eighteen minutes to walk to the café from my hostel. Plenty of time to think. My thoughts aren't straying far from Dr. Zoughbi and the work of Wi'am. "It's *ongoing* trauma, layer after layer," he had said. "There's no way that it is *post*. It's real."

My steps feel weightier as I walk with these words. It's difficult to know how to process the truth that some people's lives are so overrun with trauma that they can't begin to think of healing from it, only surviving it. I wonder how many people back home would resonate with Dr. Zoughbi's remark. How many black and brown folks in the cities. How many Indigenous people facing more land theft and forced poverty. How many closeted LGBTQ people in churches. How many undocumented immigrants watching for Immigration and Customs Enforcement officers. How many folks surviving on the streets. How many men and women incarcerated. How many parents bereaved by gun violence. How many people I don't even know I should know about. This shouldn't be anyone's world.

Rounding a corner, a sign above a door tells me I've found the meeting spot. Moran Zamir rises from a table and extends his hand to me.

"Hello, Michael," he says.

"Hi, Moran. Thanks for meeting me. Moran. Am I pronouncing that right?"

"Yes, it's fine," he says with a smile that I can't quite interpret—as in, is it actually fine or is it just not worth correcting? To me, getting someone's name right is always worth worrying about. Names and their pronunciation matter.

His green striped polo appears blue in the lamplight. We sit at a table on the sidewalk, and I order an espresso. We're the only ones here. His face is kind, and his eyes are serious. He doesn't seem too interested in small talk. I quickly get the sense that he'd like to dive in. No need to waste time.

"First of all I want to apologize for my English," he says with a bit of a sheepish smile. "It's not perfect. It's far from perfect. But it is what it is."

"It's quite good," I say, thinking how much better his English is than my Hebrew—especially since my Hebrew is a fictional concept.

"Okay," he says with a nod. A breeze rustles the leaves above us, and Human League's "Don't You Want Me" plays faintly from a café three doors down.

Moran tells me he grew up on a Jewish kibbutz near the Green Line. It was during the Oslo years in the mid-1990s— "peacetime," he calls it—and he wondered if he would even need to join the Israeli army, which is required for most citizens.

"There was lots of hope," he remembers. "People were sure that tomorrow the peace will come. And of course, this bubble completely blows in the year of 2000."

"The second intifada," I say.

"The second intifada, of course."

I remember this too. In 2000, my family was planning to move to Israel for six months during my dad's sabbatical from his medical practice in our small town of Jellico, Tennessee. We'd leave in early January 2001 and live in Jerusalem, as my dad had during his own childhood. But the end of 2000 saw the beginning of a new Palestinian uprising. Unlike the first one in the late 1980s and early 1990s—which mostly called for united civil disobedience, boycotts, and strikes—this intifada was chaotic. The sharp increase in Palestinian suicide bombings led to a sharper increase in Israeli fears. Daily newspaper headlines reported buses, night clubs, restaurants, and hotels ripped apart from bombs strapped to chests and hidden in bags. At the height of the intifada, a suicide bombing terrorized Israel almost every week. No one felt safe. Including my family. We ended up spending nearly all of that sabbatical in Greece and Europe.

"Suddenly the conflict is something that becomes really, really relevant to the daily life," Moran says. "First of all with the feeling of risk that you take any time you go to the big city. You take a bus, you go to a restaurant. I remember it was . . .

first of all, it was really terrifying. But second of all, we start to
see the Palestinian as a threat. Each one of them." He pauses.
"Each and every one of them. Let's say I go on a bus from Tel
Aviv to Beersheva, and I see one Arab guy go on this bus, then
I sit on the other side."

"Because he might have a bomb strapped to him?" I ask.

"Yeah," he says. "Or if he put his bag, you know, under the
bus, I wait until he goes on the bus, and then I check his bag."
Moran sees my raised eyebrows. "I did it," he says with a nod,
"a few times. So at one point in our mind, if we see a Palestinian or Arabic guy, we think they probably want to kill us."

"Were you encouraged to think that way by your parents,
family, friends?" I ask.

"No, my family educate me to love human being and not
to be racist. But it was the atmosphere. A lot by the media
that only told us a one-sided story. But also from the reality.
Like there was a couple that got married, and one week after
they got married, they went on the road by the kibbutz and
one Palestinian guy is waiting for nighttime and is waiting on
the road and shoots them and kills them both. It was right in
front of the gate of the kibbutz. So suddenly, it's close, not only
far away."

"There was a lot of fear," I say.

"A lot of fear," he confirms. "You feel everywhere you go
you have to look behind you. And the only thing in the world
that can keep you alive, it's the IDF. The big hero. They are the
only thing that stands between us and those people who want
to kill us. So when we look to the soldier, we look at them
and we see a hero. We want to be like that. To fight terror, to
save people."

Moran tells me it's important I understand the role of the
Israel Defense Forces in society. He says it doesn't matter

what side of the political spectrum you're on, the army stands beyond reproach.

"You can argue about this and that, but the army is off-limits," he says. "And you don't say anything bad about the soldiers or the army. And the family I grew up with was part of the Israeli *left* wing, the Zionist left, but still the army was something very important in the family tradition. Like all the men, *all* of them," he stresses, "was in combat. There's not even one man in my family, in the big family, who wasn't in combat. And that was the atmosphere I can say in general."

Moran twists his wrist, fingers outstretched, as if rotating a knob. He tells me of a shift in his thinking. He says that before joining the army, he visited Hebron as part of his year of national service. The disturbing reality of displaced Palestinians in and around the Old City produced concerns. He began questioning what was really happening, like what might those Palestinians have felt when the Israeli army forced them out of their homes and closed their shops because a Jewish settler wanted to move nearby?

"That's only one story," he says, "but when suddenly I can see something from the other side, I think that maybe the reality is more complicated. But in my mind . . ." He trails off for a moment and leans forward, elbows on the table, looking into the distance. His hands cover his mouth. "Yeah, I was eighteen years old, and in my mind, it was only like some idea that comes and goes. The picture was still there. The picture that says, 'We are the right side here. We are the justice. We protect ourselves. That's what we do. Sometimes we do not do really nice things, but we have to do it.' This picture was still there. So when I joined the army, I was sure I was doing the right thing. I always tell myself that it was good that I am there. I'm not going to do anything cruel to people; only what I need. I tell myself that it's good that you are a moral person. It's good that you are there." His hands move often as he speaks, much like mine do. A siren sounds in the distance. I imagine there must have been an incessant chorus of those in Jerusalem during the height of those horrific bombings.

Moran tells me that in 2008, the year after Hamas took control of Gaza, his military unit began operations inside the Gaza Strip—to find tunnels or a wanted combatant—and he found himself in planning meetings for these operations. Those in charge expressed one ultimate objective.

"To destroy the daily life of the population," he says.

"That was the goal of the operations?" I ask.

"The one goal," he says, "to create a feeling of fear, of threat inside the population. The main goal of all we were doing is to create this feeling inside the civilian population. The feeling of risk, that any day the army can come and destroy their house and field. I start to feel that something here is not really right. We were using really massive force, with tanks, field combatants, and with air force. They all go like a big giant. We come in and just find some village, arrest some people, bring them back. It was not in proportion. The damage was terrible. You go and destroy a house and destroy a field. For me, as someone who grew up in an agricultural community, it was terrible that we can go to an orange field with a big tractor and just crush the whole thing. Some people, that's how they make their living, how they bring food to their table. And it wasn't even part of what we're doing. It was just on the way. But what happens tomorrow with these people? What are they going to do? Maybe it's the only thing they have, these oranges that are now no longer."

These oranges that are now no longer: the sentence hangs between us. He pauses for a moment, looking at me, and I nod, encouraging him to go on.

"I can tell you a story that represents this feeling. One day, we were going to someone's house in a small village in the south of Gaza. The house was empty because all the people escaped the village. But there was one man, one guy who stayed in the house. He was handicapped. He don't have leg. And he laid down on the sofa in the living room. He can't escape. He was the only one there. We were very surprised to see him in the living room because we were sure everyone escaped. He just lie there, and he look at us, and he has no fear in his eyes. I remember. Nothing. He looked at us, and you can see desperation. It's the only thing you see.

"He talked really good Hebrew. He started talking to us, and he say, 'I used to live seven years inside Israel. I worked there in construction. I meet some Israeli Arab woman. We got married. We had three children. Then one day, after seven years, they found out I was from Gaza, and so they sent me back to Gaza. In one day. The family stayed in Israel. Then I arrived here without anything—no job, no family. One year later, there is a drone bombing in our yard one day and cut my leg off, and I became disabled. And now you come and you take all that we have, all the orange and the lemon. And I want to ask you a question: What do you want me to do? Where should I go?'"

Moran looks past me, and I can tell his eyes still see that man's face. "This question stayed with me," he says. "The people around me were saying to him, 'Oh, it's your fault. You chose Hamas.' And I thought: It has nothing to do with him. The question is not about Hamas, or Fatah. It's about something much deeper. 'Where do you want me to go now?' It was one question, one story, that started to represent something larger."

He has another story he wants to tell me. Often, the IDF would sweep into Gaza, arresting Palestinian men and boys in sight who appeared to be older than sixteen. They blindfolded, handcuffed, and carried them to the army base just outside the Gaza-Israel border. After an Israeli intelligence agent investigated them, nearly all would be released. But one day, Moran and two soldiers under his command were assigned to watch over the bound Palestinians until the intelligence agent arrived for questioning.

"We waited there in, like, a big yard with few trees," he says. "Not much shade. Really hot day. June in Gaza is not nice. There were three Palestinian guys we have to watch. One of them was really old, maybe sixty or seventy. You could see he was not healthy. So we waited there—one hour passed by, two hours, three hours. No one came. No one called. The soldiers with me started to get bored, so they started hitting the Palestinian guys. I was arguing with them about this. It was not a nice feeling. But as I told you, they had a lot of anger inside them, and they had this opportunity, and these people had their hands tied, eyes covered—they're the easiest target you can find. But anyway, in the end, they stopped. This waiting went on for hour and hour and hour, without them eating anything. We gave them water, but no food.

"And after a few hours, this old guy, he tried to say something, but I didn't understand Arabic at the time. He kept motioning to his body, and I finally realized that he needed to take a s---. He'd waited all these hours. And so I took him with me, like you take a dog, because his hands and eyes are tied, and I held him and took him around looking for a toilet. But we couldn't find one. He was really dirty, and when I asked people, no one wanted to let him use the toilet. But when I'd stop in the middle of the base to ask people, he was sure we'd arrived at a toilet, so he'd start to take off his pants. So I'd take his pants back up. It was always this.

"In the end, we find a toilet. But the whole time I had this feeling: What if *my* grandfather was like that, like an animal, like a dog? I couldn't stand it. We went back and ended up waiting from six a.m. to about six p.m. The guy from the intelligence agency called me and asked to talk to those people. He talked with them maybe two minutes in Arabic, and then told me, 'Ah, okay, you can send them back.' They waited twelve hours for two minutes, over the phone."

Moran is clearly disturbed as he recounts this memory. Honestly, I'm disturbed just listening. I'm not sure I could stand up from my chair right now if I tried. It reminds me of the horrors I saw as a volunteer chaplain in the solitary confinement units of a maximum security prison in Nashville. Binding men's hands and feet when transferring them throughout the pod. Denying them food at times. Taking all their possessions. Withholding toilet paper so they were forced to wipe with their hands. This type of humiliation and trauma can make people go crazy, make them turn to violence. I hear Dr. Zoughbi's words again—"We don't have the post-traumatic stress disorder. It's *ongoing* trauma, layer after layer."

Thankfully, these experiences produced feelings in Moran that grew "stronger and stronger." He began to feel that even if Israel was justified in protecting its citizens from Hamas's rockets in the south, its chosen method didn't feel right. Its actions were only perpetuating the cycle of violence.

"Maybe we avoid something now," Moran says, "but in the end, we just create more anger, more violence. The people we encounter probably hate us, probably want to kill us. And I can understand why. And maybe a few of them are going to try to do it. Maybe the children when they grow up. Maybe in the moment we help, but in the long picture, we just cause more damage. It's going for nowhere."

When Moran's army service ended in 2009, he could not shake this feeling. Confused, he traveled abroad to Nepal and India. He didn't know it then, but now he sees that he was trying to escape all that happened during this army service.

"And it worked for the time," he says. "I didn't really think about it. I mean, I would jump when I heard a loud noise because it reminded me of the bombing in Gaza. But mostly, I didn't think about it. But when I came back to Israel—it wasn't just one moment, it was a long process. It's hard to even put a finger on it. But the feeling starts to grow inside me that I can't just live my life and say, 'Okay, that happened. It belongs to the past. That's something that belongs to politicians. They need to find the solution.' I can't. Something is in my country that is seriously wounded, seriously not right. It has to be healed, fixed." He pauses for some time. "Again, I can't put the finger where exactly, with time; it's just a feeling that I can't just stand outside. I have to be involved in some way."

He tells me that the annual Israeli Memorial Day began to feel uncomfortable. The day was set aside for the remembrance of those who died in the Holocaust or fighting for Israel. "It's like the holy day of the relationship between the Israeli people and the IDF," he says. "A day to celebrate this holy connection. How they were a hero, and we live because of them. But since I finished the army, I can't really participate in this day. It was always a difficult day for me. I don't know where to put myself. Yeah, I am very sad on Memorial Day, of course. I know people who died in the army. Great guys. And I'm really sad they aren't here anymore. But this day isn't really for them; it's for telling young people that the army is so holy, so great. And I can't take part in this. And it was difficult to feel because in the family I grew up, it's the closest thing to a holy day that we have. As a secular family, we didn't really feel holiness. But on Memorial Day, I feel it."

"It's the same thing in the United States," I say.

"Yes, but you barbecue," he says with a laugh. "We don't. We have to be sad and serious."

I am grateful for this conversation. He's sincere and humble. The story of his journey, his struggle, has played out on his face as well as in his words. Moran tells me that the next year, he heard of a "binational Memorial Day" organized by Israelis and Palestinians, remembering the dead on both sides. Even though many in his society scoff at or even outright suspect this gathering, he decided to attend, and he heard from parents on both sides who had lost their children. They perhaps were the most justified in pursuing revenge, but they didn't. They were working together to promote peace.

"It was inspiring," he says. "I saw that the way is not to deny the pain, but to go through the pain and meet inside it—because we all share this pain."

Moran began to meet with Palestinians and hear their stories through Combatants for Peace, one of the organizations that sponsored the binational Memorial Day. He was in his midtwenties at the time, and it was the first time he met Palestinians with any kind of equality.

"I can see their point of view," he says about the meetings. "I see how much pain they have inside of them. You can see and understand that each one, every individual in Israel and Palestine, has something inside them that is wounded. Because all of us, *all of us*, in some way, suffered from this conflict. And the only way to get out of the circle of violence is by meeting each other. This is the uniqueness of Combatants for Peace. Using your personal story. Trying to make a change. And understanding that the struggle against the occupation is

not only for Palestinians. It's something that is needed for us as
Israelis, because it's killing us. Because it keeps the circle going
on and on. It's something that we have to do for us."

If he just substituted *white supremacy* for *occupation*, he'd
be preaching a sermon that I and other white Americans need
to hear. Israel's military occupation of Palestine is destroying
his country, and white supremacy is destroying mine. How
remarkable that societies pursue systems of power even
though those systems inevitably chew away at them from the
inside. The miracle is finding a way to convince our societies
that those systems have always been poison.

The café manager is taking the outside chairs inside to close
the café for the night.

"Look," Moran says, as I take out my wallet to pay for the
drinks, "the chances for peace are much less now than they
were twenty years ago, but I don't think we have another
choice. If I want to live here, I have to try to do it. That's
the place I come from. To try the best we can. The root of
violence, if you go deep into the roots, is ignorance. It's when
people are not aware of who the other people are and also
who they are themselves, at a deep level. If you build your
identity by hating the other person or being afraid of the other
person, it's something that is deep in the psychology. We must
be able to release this ignorance, this fear, and tell ourselves
that yes, there might be people that are different than me, but
they are not threats. They can be different, live a different way
of life, they can practice a different religion, but I can also live
my life and feel good about who I am without ignoring their
existence, what they're doing. The way to do this healing process—I *think*, I'm not a professional—is to go through your
personal story, like we do in Combatants for Peace. Trying to
explore why I'm afraid, what happened, what the reason this

other human being makes me afraid. And trying to do this process with yourself. If more people do this kind of thing, it will be very good for the world. I think. I *hope. Inshallah.*"

"Yes, *inshallah*," I say. God willing.

4

YOU MAY NOT KILL IN MY SON'S NAME

What's your definition of forgiveness?" This is one of the first questions Robi Damelin asks me.

I stammer for a second while she smiles and takes off her sunglasses. "You think you can ask *me* questions, *habibi* [my dear] . . ." she says, in a way that makes it clear this will be less an interview and more a conversation. The server sets my Americano down on the glass table between us.

Robi has always struck me as someone who cuts straight through the fat of any conversation, as if her life doesn't have room for superficiality and chitchat. But she's not a cold person—far from it. The kindness of her eyes and the warmth of her presence help to calm the intimidation I feel sitting with such a remarkable woman. I learned of Robi's story of bereavement and bravery through the documentary *Encounter*

Point, the same one that introduced me to Ali Abu Awwad. I learned how her son David was serving as an officer in the Israeli army in 2002 when a Palestinian sniper shot and killed him at a West Bank checkpoint. I saw in that film her refusal to be owned by a desire for vengeance.

Robi is the Israeli spokesperson for the organization Ali mentioned, the Parents Circle-Families Forum.[1] The organization is a beautiful collection of bereaved and resilient Palestinians and Israelis who travel their country, region, and world witnessing to the transformative potential of meeting rather than killing those on the other side. They host dialogues between people of both nations, engage young people in schools to encourage them to take a different path than dehumanizing the other, and even hold joint Memorial Day celebrations, like the one Moran told me about. Much of my story-gathering project left room for unexpected meetings and impromptu conversations, but this time with Robi was one I made sure to plan.

Robi and I go back and forth for a bit, exchanging various definitions of forgiveness. We consider some of the common questions: Does forgiveness require reconciliation? Should the offender be remorseful to receive forgiveness? Does forgiving mean giving up your right to justice? Does forgiveness mean forgetting? Having recently written a book on this subject, I'm loving this conversation.[2] And I am listening carefully to Robi as she speaks about forgiveness because for her, it isn't hypothetical. It's held in her body. My friend Pádraig Ó Tuama once said to me, "Some people's theories are other people's trauma." That's how it is with Robi. None of this is academic; it's actual life.

---

1. For more information, see www.theparentscircle.org.
2. See Michael T. McRay, *Where the River Bends: Considering Forgiveness in the Lives of Prisoners* (Eugene, OR: Cascade Books, 2015).

"The most meaningful definition for me," Robi says, "was one I got from a South African woman whose daughter had been killed, and she has today an organization for ex-combatants with the guy who sent the people to kill her daughter. And she'd gone to the Truth and Reconciliation Commission, and she said to the people who'd killed her daughter, the *actual* people who'd killed her daughter, 'I forgive you.' I wanted to know what she meant. You haven't seen my film *One Day after Peace*?"

"Not yet. I've seen *Encounter Point*."

"Oh, no, *Encounter Point* is way back," she laughs. "*One Day after Peace* was when I went to South Africa to look at the Truth and Reconciliation Commission to see what lessons to learn, to explore forgiving, and see my own s---. I met her. She's Afrikaans, white—the last person you'd expect to have any relationship with black people. And I said to her, 'What do you mean when you said you forgive them? What does that mean?' So she said to me that forgiving is giving up your just right to revenge. For her, that's what it meant. Then I met the guy who sent the people to kill her daughter, expecting to meet this monster. He turned out to be the most extraordinary man in total integrity, and he said, 'By her forgiving me, she has released me from the prison of my inhumanity.' What more do you want than that? So I don't know what forgiving is. I just know that what she said was really meaningful for me."

ROBI SPENT HER CHILDHOOD in South Africa, and I ask her to tell me about it. She says, "I remember that there was a horse that the guy from the dairy used to deliver milk on, and the guy used to beat the horse. And I'm a major animal lover, and I was five. And I remember that I went with my friend Barbara Fudge—I remember her name to this day, with ginger hair and freckles—and we went and we stole the horse and brought it home to my house. Of course we had no idea what we'd do with a horse, so we put it in the tennis court. When my father came home and found a horse in the tennis court, you can imagine how thrilled he was. But that's the beginning of understanding that you can be a part of change. And then I got sent to boarding school because I was so naughty," she laughs and sticks her tongue out. "How naughty can you be at six? Pretty naughty, I suppose."

"How long were you in South Africa?" I ask her.

"Until 1967. I grew up in South Africa. I came to save Israel from the war and ended up working in a chicken house. But the chickens were very violent," she says with a grin.

"NOW ONE OF THE THINGS I was going to ask you," I say to Robi, "was about how you made the decision after David was killed to choose the path you are on now. It sounds like in some ways your life of social justice and anti-apartheid work and so on had already made that decision for you."

"One of the first things I said to the army when they came to my door after David was killed was, 'Don't kill anyone in David's name.'"

I remember that line from hearing her tell that story in the *Encounter Point* documentary. Officers appear at her door, a visit every parent of a soldier dreads. They tell her that her son has been killed, and what does she say? "You may not kill anyone in my son's name." I've never forgotten the courage of such a response—the way she immediately and instinctively set about to disrupt the cycles of violence.

Two or three months later, Robi was asked to speak at a huge peace demonstration, in front of thousands of people.

People had heard of her demand that no more killing happen in her son's name, and now they wanted to hear her in person. As she stood waiting to speak, she had no idea what she was going to say.

"And I remember I was standing down at the bottom," she tells me. "I'd been to a psychologist after David was killed, and it took me . . . in the beginning I was running around the world, so I went to India to an ashram and, you know, just all kinds of mad things."

"Peace-related things or—?" I ask.

"No, nothing. I just wanted to get away from being public property. Because it's such a small country, and there was so much written about David because David was really quite a special person and had an enormous following of students and all kinds of stuff. So I went with David's girlfriend to an ashram in Pune, [India,] which was like going into another world, completely. But when I came back, I realized I can't keep running away. I've got to face myself. I knew I wanted to do something. I had no idea what it was, but I knew I wanted to do something that would stop this madness and prevent other people from this pain. But I didn't know what yet.

"And Yitzhak Frankenthal came to see me, together with Roni Hirshenson, and they'd seen a lot of stuff that was about me that was in the paper because I'd called the children of the settlers 'abused'—you can imagine how popular I was after that. But they *are* abused! And each generation that grows up there becomes worse abusers than their parents. You can't bring up a child that goes to school in a tank or has permission to throw stones at little children and imagine that he will not be an abuser even worse than his parents. So I wrote from this—right from the beginning I said what was on my mind. I'd gone to the psychologist because I didn't know what to do with myself. And she said to me—well, first, it was unbeliev-ably boring. I thought, 'Geez, I've been there and done that. I can't sit here and listen to this crap about my parents five hundred years after I've settled it all. It's nothing to do with them anymore.' So the second time I came she said to me, 'Listen, you know, I don't think I can do anything for you. You will do big things.' And she said, 'You will have no fear.' So I said, 'What do you mean?' And I was very angry. And she said, 'Because what else can happen to you?'

"So I went away, and I was absolutely mad as a snake with her. But it took time, and the day that I stood up at that thing, I said, 'You know, she's right. I don't have any fear.' It's not because I think I'm so remarkable. It's because I really believe in what I'm saying, and I don't care if you don't like what I'm saying. That was a kind of turning point to kind of understand where I was, and I got more and more involved in Parents Circle, and it overtook my life."

Robi pauses for a moment and glances to the side before returning her gaze to me. She says, "Then I started to think about the culpability of victims, and that is another story."

I nod. "That is very tricky territory to walk into."

"One day I was at a conference about *love* and *forgive-ness*," Robi says. She exaggerates the words in a bit of playful mockery. "You know, all these rainbows and flowers and bad poetry." We both laugh at this.

She adjusts her scarf a bit. "At that same conference, there was a Jesuit monk, and he started talking about the culpability of victims, and I got furious. I'd never heard that term before. I was so angry. 'What do you mean the culpability of victims? How dare you!' Most people immediately see rape, you know, so I went home and I couldn't sleep the whole night. And I was like, 'Geez, you know, he's right. I mean, my child was in uniform. It's not that he was totally innocent. And why did I let him?' Well, I couldn't stop him, but maybe I could have stopped him from going into the occupied territories even though he didn't want to go himself.

"And so you realize that there is a culpability—that if David was in uniform, this man shot him not because he was *David*. These are things that are really difficult to process. It's fighting with yourself, you know, and thinking about why this man killed David, and knowing that when this man was a little boy, he saw his uncle very violently killed by the Israeli army. These are the things that happen."

I understand why Robi doesn't talk much about this publicly. It's a risky conversation. Most people like the world to be binary: You're either a perpetrator or a victim. We don't want messy ideas. Our brains are wired to sort people into categories. Early in human history, we had to do this to know whether something was friend or foe. We still do it, in lots of ways. Dichotomies are easier to engage than complexities.

But I'm with Robi—the world just isn't that simple. Studying in Belfast and visiting people in prison for years made this clear to me. Almost always, a perpetrator was a victim first, and *sometimes*, victims are targeted because they were either actual or perceived perpetrators themselves. I am struck by Robi's integrity in acknowledging the culpability of her own child.

It's important for me to say here that part of responsibly engaging complexity around the blurred lines of perpetrator and victim is to use wise discernment. Clearly, for Robi to suggest that her son David, a soldier in a military occupying others' lands and lives, might bear culpability in his own death is not the same as suggesting that a woman is responsible for being sexually assaulted because of her outfit. Nor is it to suggest that a kid like Tamir Rice is partly to blame for being killed by Cleveland police. He's not culpable, and neither is the woman. Sometimes, victims are just victims. And sometimes, it's more complicated than that.

Peace isn't built through bumper-sticker slogans and pleasant conversations. Peace is a difficult, painful, and complex journey.

After Robi had traveled extensively to demonstrate the power of dialogue, meeting the enemy, and pursuing reconciliation rather than revenge, she found herself faced with an opportunity to test her own commitment to the work. The Israeli army had caught the Palestinian combatant who killed David. She had to decide whether she actually believed the sermons she'd been preaching. This is where the rubber met the road.

Robi decided to write to the man, now in an Israeli prison. "I want to meet this guy and do a completion, more for myself than him," she says to me. This is where the story left off in the film *Encounter Point*. At the end of the film, she tries to set up a meeting and receives no response.

"Then after we made the film I went to meet his lawyer. And the lawyer went to the judge to tell him who I was and all, and he said, okay, he's willing to meet me. And then I got furious. 'What do you mean he's willing to meet me? He killed *my son*. What do you mean *he's* willing to meet *me*?' And that's your immediate emotion that comes out. But I decided that there's something bigger than me in this whole event."

Despite her efforts, the encounter never happened. To this day, Robi remains open to meeting the man who stole her son from her. She maintains that if he had *known* David, and didn't only see him as a soldier, he never could have killed him.

"You see, you don't know who the person is behind the gun. I say this all the time, everywhere I go. About two and a half years after David was killed, I was giving a talk at the American embassy, and this Palestinian was sitting in the audience, and he kept looking at me, and I knew he wanted to say something, so I went to him and I said, 'What?' And he said, 'I just wanted to tell you that the day before your son was killed, I drove through that checkpoint and this very tall'—David was 6'3" or something—'this tall guy came and said, "Look, I'm very sorry but I have to check your papers. It's my duty. It's like paying income tax, and I'll do it as fast as I can."' And they got into a conversation, a very long conversation, apparently, and the man said to me, 'The next day, when I heard your son was killed, I was so sorry.' And there's the essence of all the work that we're doing, because he and David exchanged their humanities."

"DO YOU KNOW of our narrative project?" Robi asks me.

"No, I don't," I say, feeling a bit self-conscious about how out of date I seem to be with the work of the Parents Circle.

"When it started off," Robi says, leaning forward, "it was called History through the Human Eye. What happened was we recognized in our group that we all had a sympathy with each other because we shared the same pain. But that didn't mean that we agreed with one another from the national level, from the interpretation of facts, or even our personal narratives. So we decided, okay, that if we really want to trust each other, we've got to find out. So there were 140 of us—70 Palestinians and 70 Israelis. That's a lot. And we decided the first thing we'll do, we'll go to the Holocaust Museum. That's not for comparison of suffering, but if you don't understand that part of Jewish history, you'll never understand the DNA of fear.

"So we went, thinking that 70 Palestinians coming to the Holocaust Museum is already a big step. They don't really want to come to the Holocaust Museum; having to look at somebody else's pain, that's not easy. But we went and then had this huge lunch afterwards, all of us, and then we had a lecture by a Palestinian historian and by an Israeli historian, each one giving the milestones of our history. So it would be 1948 for us, our independence. And the Nakba for them, '67, '73, the two intifadas—and each side, each historian, gave their interpretation. Now, you don't all become Gandhi by the end of it, but you understand how the other person sees their history, which is a very big step toward some kind of conflict resolution.[3]

"So that was that," she says. "And then the next day we go to a [Palestinian] village." She trails off for a moment as the voices of two young women at the table behind us grow louder than seems necessary. Robi sighs and gets a mischievous glimmer in her eyes.

"Wait, I just have to glare at them." She slowly turns and does just that. The women are unfazed. Robi turns back, smirking, "They didn't take any notice of me."

"That was amazing," I say, laughing in a kind of delighted shock. Robi laughs too, with a full-chested laugh that keeps us smiling a little longer. It's in this moment that I love her. Not because Robi is spectacular, but because she is inspiringly ordinary.

"Anyway," she goes on, "the next day we go to this village. Two [Palestinian] families come from this village, which was Palestine before 1948, and now is in Israel. We get there; there's

---

3. For a short primer on the history of this conflict, see Martin P. Bunton, *The Palestinian-Israeli Conflict: A Very Short Introduction* (Oxford, UK: Oxford University Press, 2013).

nothing left, you know. We find just the dome of a mosque."
It's important to know that in the months during and before
Israel's war of independence, over five hundred Palestinian
villages were depopulated and razed. The village they were
visiting that day was one of them. "One of the mothers started
to cry and said, 'See, this is the well I used to draw water out
of as a child.' And so you begin to understand the longing."

Here again, I'm seeing the power of empathy. Through
careful, humanizing encounters with others, our worldviews
can shift. They expand—sometimes moving like a glacier and
sometimes like an avalanche—making room for another's
experience to hold true alongside our own. Empathy has a lot
to do with understanding, with comprehending the story of
someone else and honoring it as valid and important, even if
it challenges our own. Empathy can be a driving force behind
tremendous change. As Robi said, it can facilitate the resolution of conflict.

Building empathy for the sake of empathy, however, isn't
enough. It should lead to compassionate action for improving
the world. This is what Ali was talking about. Empathy that
does not lead toward constructive efforts for personal and
social improvement isn't of much use to anyone. Robi knows
this, too, and she tells me that part of their narrative project
is the creation of some collaborative effort by those involved.

"ONE OF THE CRITIQUES I've often heard of this kind of work,"
I say to Robi, "is that there seems to be an assumption that
justice and reconciliation are in tension with one another." I
tell her about the Palestinian professor in Nablus who wrote
me the email saying, "This is an inappropriate conversation."
"I wonder if you all get critiques of the Parents Circle about

whether the emphasis on talking is perpetuating the problem. Something Ali said that has stuck with me is that dialogue for him is a means toward his liberation, and if it's not, then it's a tool of his oppression."

"Yes, that's wise. You know, dialogue is not hummus and hugging. It's not. It's very painful and can lead to severe arguments. But when I look at the Parents Circle as a group, we've gone through some really tough times. Tough times in that it wasn't an equal situation. It was more a patronizing, Israeli situation. But today we're in a completely different place. We've got two offices, two directors. It's like Noah's Ark. We've got two of everything."

"Would you use language of justice to talk about the Parents Circle, that you all are doing justice work?"

"No," she says, without much hesitation. "No, because what is justice work? We say, 'Get out of the occupied territories,' obviously. But I think it's also important *for Israel* that we get out, *more important* for Israel, actually, in the long run. If the Palestinians have a lot of patience, they can just wait until we ruin *ourselves*. And I say this all the time, even if you don't care about the Palestinians—and I care deeply—if you understand how the occupation is affecting the moral fiber of this country, then you must realize that we have to end this."

I GLANCE AT MY PHONE to check the time. We've talked longer than I told her we would.

"I know it's time to close this conversation," I say. "As a parting question, I'd be interested in knowing what—in this time of political despair—what gives you hope?"

"I can't afford to give up," she says simply. "I live here. I can't give up hope. If I give up hope, why am I staying here? I could go and live in London with my fancy cousins and play golf; I don't know. It's for the future of my grandchildren. I look at them, and I can't believe that I might not have done everything I possibly could to stop this madness. And I'm not so arrogant to think that I'm that important, but I know that what we're *doing* is very important. So it isn't about giving up hope. It isn't about fear. It's about knowing that when you believe in something—and I really, with all my heart, believe in what I'm doing—I can't stop."

I take a breath, smile, and place my hand on my heart. "Thank you so much for your time, Robi," I say.

"Of course, *habibi*," she says, and she rises from the table, hugs me tight, and walks away, down Remez Street, toward whatever comes next.

5

FORTUNATELY, IT WAS PARADISE

hall I?" he asks. We're sitting on the stone veranda of his hilltop home sipping tea, the one thing he actually knows how to make. His striped polo shirt is buttoned up to his neck to block the breeze.

"If you're willing," I say. I'm just being deferential; I know he's willing. He's always delighted to recite English poetry. He loves the attention, and he loves pretending he's shy about it.

His voice is unforgettable, which makes the poetry even better. He's exaggerated yet authentic. Larger than life but perfectly himself. In everyday conversations, he crescendos and decrescendos with almost every sentence. At times, I jolt back in my chair when his voice bursts into a kind of shouting, and then I lean in when he drops to a hush.

"Yes?" he asks again, smiling with satisfaction. But he doesn't need another answer. His humility is finished; he's ready for Shakespeare.

"Under the greenwood tree / Who loves to lie with me, / And turn his merry note / Unto the sweet bird's throat, / Come hither, come hither, come hither: / Here shall he see / No enemy / But winter and rough weather."

On he goes with this Shakespearean song—with a verse on ambition, food, and pleasure. The refrain comes round again: "Come hither, come hither, come hither: / Here shall he see / No enemy / But winter and rough weather."

I rest in my chair, contented. I've heard him do this dozens of times over the past decade, and I never grow tired of it. This aging Palestinian man sits enthroned in a plastic chair on his own porch, on his own land. He's surrounded by military occupation. He has stories of trauma and suffering and discrimination. Some days, the sorrow drips from him as if he'd just swum in it. And still, he always ends his Shakespeare the same way—with his own peaceful note: "And yes, I hope we shall see no enemy here, but winter and rough weather. Believe me, we want no enemy. We want only to live in peace with our neighbors." Sometimes I think he says it because he believes it; sometimes, because he *wants* to believe it, and the reminder helps.

He lets out a heavy sigh toward the Judean hills, as if his breath might bless the land stretching from his fruit trees to the Jordanian mountains on the horizon.

"Yes," he says, almost like a whisper.

ABDULLAH AND NOHA AWWAD live in paradise. That's what they tell anyone who pulls into their driveway in Beit Sahour, a small town next to Bethlehem.

"Welcome to my paradise!" Abdullah calls, arms outstretched. I step out of the car, smiling already as the gate
closes behind me. I'm happy to be back in this place that feels
so much like home. The Awwads' paradise has been my Palestinian home for years. I've stayed with them at least once on
every trip over the past decade.

When I interned with Christian Peacemaker Teams (CPT)
in Hebron in 2012, the daily burden of the occupation drained
and depressed me—which was nothing compared to the pain
of those who face it as a way of life. Every couple of weeks, I
escaped the weight of Hebron for the paradise of the Awwads'
home. I would sit out on the veranda in the morning, pick-
ing kumquats from a garden tree, scraping freshly made jams
on my toast, and sipping Arabic coffee. Abdullah and Noha
would often keep me company.

"We worry about you, our son," Noha would say.

"Yes, you must be careful, Michael," Abdullah would add.
"Believe me, you must be careful!" It felt good to have them
care, made me feel safer. Their welcome has always been real.
Like their paradise.

The Awwads' stone home sits on a hill. The whole place
is beautiful, filled with a kind of infectious joy. Potatoes,
greens, herbs, and flowers grow in soil held tight by tiered,
waist-high walls. Orange, fig, lemon, and olive trees sur-
round the house. The Awwads grow grapes for sweet wine
and jam. Their veranda is wide and long enough to seat large
numbers of guests around a table while their young grandchildren bike in circles around the meal. Their home is what
I imagine the garden of Eden to look like—just with a patio
and gated driveway.

Abdullah is proud of the home they built together. And he
loves to tell me the story.

Abdullah was born in British-occupied Palestine in 1942, six years before Israel became a state. He doesn't remember much about those early years except gunfire and refugees. When the 1967 war struck, Abdullah was living in Turkey, studying English literature at Ankara University. After finishing his degree, he tried to return home but learned that "everything was occupied." So occupied, in fact, that he spent two years in Jordan applying for a family reunion visa so he could see his family. Abdullah couldn't see a future for himself in Palestine at that time, so he moved to Libya and worked for a television broadcasting company.

Abdullah thrived in his job, so much so that the newly in-power Muammar Gaddafi approached Abdullah to come work for him. He needed the news of the world translated from English into Arabic, and Abdullah's English skills and work ethic made him valuable. For several years, Abdullah translated the daily report of world happenings for Gaddafi and his military council, and he was well compensated. While in Libya, Abdullah met Noha—a Palestinian from Gaza—and they married and had two sons. After seven years, Abdullah and Noha knew they needed to leave. One night in 1976, they fled Libya with their sons and all the money they'd made from Gaddafi. They never looked back.

Abdullah and Noha returned to their roots in Palestine, settling in Abdullah's hometown of Beit Sahour. Here they built their paradise. Abdullah smiles at me and jokes, "I built this house with Gaddafi's money," as if to say that even a dictator's money can be redeemed toward beauty.

MAHMOUD DARWISH IS WIDELY REGARDED as the national poet of Palestine. His prolific poetry springs from the lips of most any Palestinian, from farmer to Fatah leader, baker to banker. Everyone knows Darwish, born in 1941. Even after his death in 2008, many Palestinians regard him as the voice of the people. His poems hold both a sorrow and beauty. Even the English translations of his original Arabic sound magical. He conveyed with such precise language the longing of life in exile, of how it feels to be a refugee dreaming of home.

Sitting on a shelf in my home library is a collection of his called *Unfortunately, It Was Paradise*. I won't quote any lines, since it's far too expensive to get permission to quote poetry in a book. But it's the title that grips me anyway: *Unfortunately, It Was Paradise*. When I read these four words, I can hear Darwish and other exiled Palestinians I know saying with pain something like, "Maybe it would be easier to let go of Palestine if there were nothing remarkable about it. Maybe it could have been easier to lose our homeland, become refugees, witness someone else move into our houses, and eat our food. But unfortunately, it was paradise. We can never let it go."

These four words also hold the story of the Awwads for me, or at least part of their story. After years of the Israeli government denying access to their birthland, and finding steady employment abroad, how easy it might have been to stay gone. They could have let go of Palestine and moved on, as so much of the world did. But unfortunately, it was paradise.

WHEN ABDULLAH'S FAMILY RETURNED home, they considered how best to take care of their homeland. "I wanted to *do* something," Abdullah says to me, "to do something for reconciliation. So I helped start a center called the Palestine Centre for Rapprochement between People. Between the Israelis and

Palestinians. And we invited many Israelis to come. 'Let's talk.' And many of them came."

His tone rises a bit. "Believe me, my friend, I'll tell you very frankly: as long as there is occupation, as long as there are settlements, as long as there is annexation of the land, there will be no peace between the Arabs and the Israelis. Peace comes when each party takes what it deserves: its rights. And I think we have the right in Jerusalem, we have the right in the West Bank, we have the right to live a decent life. I built my house with my own sweat, and I think I have the right to live in it."

When Abdullah names his right to be in his home, I know he's not being dramatic.

I've seen a Palestinian family made homeless by the IDF. It was February 2012. A family of ten or so stood in the rubble of their home in the south Hebron hills. An Israeli bulldozer hummed not far away, close to the settlement looking to expand into the area where this family lived. It was the second time the IDF had demolished their home.[1]

"There must be people in Israel who must be farsighted to think of peace between the Palestinians and the Israelis, and the sooner the better," Abdullah says. "Because extremism and fundamentalism are growing among Palestinians, and among Arabs, and among Muslims, and among Jews. The more it takes, you know, the more complicated it becomes." I think he means the more it takes root, and he's right. The move toward extremes is catching fire around the globe, including in the United States. "Israel must realize," he goes on, "that building walls eight meters high will not bring her peace. The only

---

1. To read more about this story, see Michael T. McRay, "The Powers of Destruction," in *Letters from "Apartheid Street": A Christian Peacemaker in Occupied Palestine* (Eugene, OR: Cascade Books, 2013), 34–36.

way to bring peace is to build bridges of friendship, of peace, between Israel and its neighbors. That is the only way."

"NOW, WHEN YOU CAME BACK, why did you decide to work for reconciliation?" I ask him. "Because you were denied for two years after college being able to see your family, Noha can't visit Gaza—you have a lot of reasons to hate Israel and to want to fight back. Many people in the States look at Palestinians and think that's what you do. So why did you choose a different way?"

I love his answer. "I am a Christian believer," he starts, his voice full of conviction, "and my Lord told me, 'Love your enemy.' I am a pacifist. I taught my children to be pacifists. I don't like bloodshed. I don't like anybody to be killed, whether Palestinian or Israeli. We are *all* the children of God. And I think that God loves me as he loves any Israeli. So we want to live together, side by side."

He's preaching now, and it's a sermon I'd listen to every Sunday. Especially because I share his faith, his conviction to love enemies, his commitment to nonviolence. In many ways, these are the foundations upon which I've sought to build a meaningful life. And this foundation is part of what led me to Hebron with CPT, to serve as a chaplain in a maximum security prison, to study reconciliation and conflict transformation, and even to pursue this project.

"The only thing," Abdullah continues, "is you cannot just sit fold-handed and do nothing. You have to *work* for peace. When we sit together side by side, face-to-face, on the same level, we can understand each other. And the more we understand each other, the closer we become. The only way to live in peace is to give each one his rights. And I think I have the right to live with dignity and with self-respect in my home, in my town, with my children, and till the soil and build bridges of friendship and peace with the other side."

THERE ARE MANY PLACES I love in Israel and Palestine. In fact, some of the places I love most in the world are on that land between the Jordan River and Mediterranean Sea. Jerusalem's Old City. The shores of the Sea of Galilee. The Awwads' paradise. Sunset at an old Roman aqueduct near Caesarea, where my late grandfather excavated as an archaeologist. But most days, I'll tell you that my favorite place of all is the Al Basma Centre.

When Abdullah returned to Palestine, he paid attention to the unmet needs of his hometown. And he decided to "do something." So a few years after his return, he formed and led a committee to address the high rate of developmental disabilities in and around his community of Beit Sahour. Beit Sahour, after all, means "house of vigilance" in Arabic.

"We had six cases, first," he tells me, and his eyes are already smiling thinking about Al Basma. "It was 1983, and these six cases, we sat on the floor. We had one room, no chairs, no tables at all, but we meant *to serve*. And where there's a will, there is always a way, Michael. And we have the will. And we wanted to serve our community. By time, people realize we are serious about this. And the center started to grow."

Today, the Al Basma Special Rehabilitation Centre welcomes upward of thirty-five to forty "students," as they're called. Some are teenagers; others are middle-aged. I've visited Al Basma on every trip I've made to Palestine since 2007. In the summer of 2010, I volunteered for two months at the center with two college friends. It was one of my most meaningful summers.

Each day I walked through the doors of the center, the same sounds greeted me. Rushdi joyfully shouting, "Miiiiike!" eyes wide with love; Nizaar bellowing his random operatic serenades; Senna shuffling in to tell me, "*Bahebak*, I love you"; Jamla's voice calling out "Breakfast!" as the students whipped chairs and tables around to prepare to eat. Then there were the enthusiastic farewells from the students as they hustled to the bus when its horn sounded at one thirty in the afternoon, and the constant calls of "*Habibi*! My love, my friend!"

That summer, my friends and I did everything with the students, despite our inability to communicate much with words. It turns out, love and laughter go a long way toward working well together. Some days, we all made greeting and Christmas cards from recycled paper. Some days, we worked in the garden. Other days, we sat with the students while they made olive wood ornaments and then helped them collect the sawdust to make fuel to heat the center. We sat in music therapy circles with them and applauded their theater productions.[2]

And we danced. Every day. I soon realized I'd never truly danced until I found myself in a dance-off with Issa, a young man with a variation of Down syndrome. The familiar beats of Arabic pop music would blare, and I'd be doing simple steps (the kind of moves I learned from Will Smith in *Hitch*), laughing with Khalil or Muhammad, and then I'd catch sight of him. Issa would lock eyes with me, and I'd know immediately he meant business. He'd start toward me, gritting his teeth and shaking his shoulders like he was doing the milkshake. I couldn't back down from this challenge if I wanted to stay in his good graces. I had to learn to dance well fast, or he was going to mop the floor with me. A circle would form around

---

2. Today, the center also grows parsley and other vegetables in aquaponics gardens to sell to local markets. They heat the building with solar panels.

us. Yells of excitement cheered us on. And we danced, back
and forth, trying to one-up the other with some special move.
I know in Issa's mind, and probably in most of the others, he
always won. He'd clasp my hand with a big slap to congrat-
ulate me on a battle well fought. The party would rage on as
Issa retired to a chair, triumphant.

Issa's origin story always stays with me. I've heard Abdullah tell his version of it more times than I can count. Not long
after the center opened, Abdullah and his colleagues received
word that a young boy had been left in a cave. He could not
function on his own, and the angels of Al Basma rescued him
and brought him to the center. They taught him to feed and
clothe himself, to speak and to write. Then they discovered he
had a talent: weaving on the loom. Issa has become a master
weaver. To this day, he crafts beautiful rugs for the center to
sell. My wife and I have a couple of them in our home.

I've never been part of anything that contained as much joy
as Al Basma. It will forever hold a special place in my heart. It
is where I learned that intimacy doesn't need conversation. It
is where I learned the depth of forms of communication other
than language, and of languages other than those spoken or
written. It is where I learned that all one really needs for soul
connection is presence, attention, and affection. And it's where
I learned that without the ability to speak a full sentence to
one another, you can build trust simply by showing up and
coming back.

And every time I come back, I am wrapped in the arms
of humans who have resurrected, like Issa. People previously
considered useless, embarrassing, and unnecessary are now full
of life. They feel as if they are contributing to their community,
to a better Beit Sahour, a better Palestine, a better world. At
Al Basma, I am held by the hands of beautiful people who just

needed room to realize they are acceptable just as they are. I feel at home in their company. And through all the kisses and saliva, each visit is like another baptism into hope and love.

It's not only the work of the center that is remarkable; it's also who is doing it. The center is run by a small group of inspirational women, both Christian and Muslim. Many months of the year, the center falls short of the funds needed to operate. Rather than risk shutting it all down, the women volunteer to take pay cuts from already thin salaries. "What will happen to the students if they can't come here?" Basma, the director, asked me one day. "They need this place."

And I've seen what she means. The students *love* the center. "It's like a beehive," Abdullah tells me. "Everybody's working, everybody's smiling." To see such community, such collaboration, is good news in times of such fear and animosity. Because Al Basma tells me that religion and difference need not be markers of division. It's not written in stone anywhere that hospitality and affection shall be suspended in the company of difference. In fact, it's in the presence of difference that hospitality is often most needed.

IN THE SUMMER OF 2010, when my college friends and I volunteered with Al Basma, we met a young Palestinian Muslim woman named Tamara. Because of our language barriers, we were unable to communicate much with her. We mostly drank tea, worked on crafts, and smiled. One day, she sent word that she wanted to host us in her family's home for dinner. We accepted, obviously—home-cooked Palestinian cuisine is not to be missed.

Entering off a side street, we climbed a winding set of stone stairs to reach her family's home. Their house was simple. As far as I could tell it contained only two rooms, both some-what spartan, with a few pictures and small woven tapestries hanging on the walls. Outside these rooms was a stone porch of sorts. Grapevines grew over their doorway, and a few steep steps led to a pathway connecting the roof of Tamara's house to her grandmother's.

Our hosts greeted us in the traditional Palestinian manner: "*Ahlan wasahlan*, you are most welcome." They invited us to sit while Tamara's father, Muhammad, prepared our meal. On an old tin cooking tray, he layered chicken, sliced potatoes, tomatoes, carrots, and large chunks of eggplant. He covered the food with three or four local spices and then placed the dish in an ancient-looking rooftop stove.

When the dinner finished cooking, he removed it with care using blocks of olive wood that doubled as oven mitts. He set the tray of food in the center of the narrow outdoor porch, and we all sat around it. Tamara handed us pieces of pita, which we used to pick up bites from the tray.

I looked around me as we started eating. Three white American Christian young men and six brown Palestinian Muslims sat cross-legged in a circle around a meal, eating from one central dish. Muhammad said, "Here, in Palestine, we all eat together. Not like in America. Each does not have his own plate here. We eat as one."

Throughout that night, we received tea and coffee, as well as lessons from the Qur'an, insights into life under occupation, and questions about some of the mysteries of the Christian faith. At one point Muhammad asked, "What is a Muslim? A Muslim," he continued, answering his own question, "a *true* Muslim, is someone who does not hurt someone else. Not with the body, and not with the words. This is a Muslim. The Qur'an teaches this."

He told us that when we understand the heart of Islam, we may start to see that it is a religion of peace, of respect for others, and of devotion to God. He pointed out that as with Christianity, Judaism, and other religions, the fundamentalists of Islam abuse its teachings, hijacking popular opinion and reducing the nobility of Islam into something sinister.

He told us, "We are all brothers. The Jewish, the Christians, and the Muslims. All brothers. We have the same ancestors and all worship the same God. We are all one."

After hours of welcome and conversation, we stood to leave, saying farewell to the family and thanking them for their gracious hospitality. Muhammad took our hands in his. His firm grip comforted me. He looked to each of us and said, "You must come back to see me before you leave. You must. You are like my sons."

I knew, as he closed the door to their home, that his words weren't the answer to all the ills of the world. But I remember thinking they might be a good start.[3]

ABDULLAH AND I LEAVE his hillside home and drive down into town to buy produce for dinner. On the way, he pulls onto a side street and into the driveway of a home I've never visited. It belongs to one of his friends—an olive wood carver who sells handmade nativity sets out of his garage. I cannot imagine how he could earn enough money out here to support his family. This home shop isn't close to the tourist areas of Bethlehem. You would come out to buy from him only if you already knew where he was.

"Yes, okay, Michael," Abdullah says, heading for the car, "wait here and see his work, and I'll return from the market

---

3. A version of this story first appeared on the former website OnFaith on April 3, 2017.

soon." Abdullah speeds away—he always drives too fast—and I turn back to the man and his son, who assists him.

I quickly realize they speak almost no English, and I regrettably speak minimal Arabic. We do a lot of pointing, motioning with hands, and using short simple words. He sits and demonstrates how he makes the nativity sets. The craftmanship is impressive. He takes great care with every piece—the measuring, shaping, cutting, sanding. It's all so precise.

His garage is full of unsold nativity sets. If he's discouraged, he doesn't show it. He just continues to make more. I see one that I love. It's small and profound. The holy family rests in a stable while the wise men approach from the left. Except, in this scene, they cannot reach Jesus; Israel's separation wall blocks their journey.

I assume Abdullah has brought me here so I can patronize his friend's shop. I do not intend to disappoint. "*Adesh*?" I ask. I've taken enough taxis and bought enough stuff in Palestine to know the Arabic term for "How much?"

"Free," he says.

"*Shu*? What?" I ask, thinking he's used a wrong word.

"Free," he says again. "Abdullah's friend, my friend." And I realize that he's shown enough hospitality to strangers to know the English words for "This is a gift."

I am sure I look stunned. I put my hand over my heart, nod to him, and say, "*Shukran ktiir*, thank you very much." I've always received legendary hospitality in the Holy Land. But this man has never met me, and given his location, I suspect I may be his only customer of the day. But it doesn't matter. Because I'm the friend of his friend, he wants to be generous.

Abdullah's friend reminds me of Mahmoud Abu Eid. Mahmoud's father and my grandfather were friends. My grandfather was an archaeologist and Mahmoud's father,

Jamil, was an antiquities dealer in Jerusalem. They met in the late 1960s, and while their relationship was primarily professional, the deep respect and affection between them was anything but. For thirty years, they visited each other every time my grandparents traveled to the Old City. I've watched tears form in Jamil's eyes whenever my grandfather's name crossed his lips.

Mahmoud and my father, David, are like brothers today. When they first met in February 2000, Mahmoud hurried to embrace my dad. He said, "This very day your father's name was spoken in my home. And because my father loves your father, it is your obligation to let me do everything I can to help you." For Mahmoud, love created generous responsibilities.

WHEN ABDULLAH RETURNS from the market, we drive back to paradise, and I set my new nativity scene in my room next to my bag. Noha is preparing stuffed grape leaves, one of my favorite Middle Eastern dishes.

The three of us eat together. There's such peace here around this table. I sigh with delight, thinking of all the years left to sit around this table with this couple who is like family to me. One day I hope to bring my wife and children, and we'll pick dates together in this garden of Eden.

We finish dinner, and I rise to help Noha clean. She scolds me, with love, "Sit, my son. You are our guest."

Abdullah leans back. "Yes," he says, his go-to filler word. He gazes at his home, his orchards, and the hills across the horizon.

"We must have hope, Michael," he says at last, turning toward me. "We hope that one day we will have peace in the land of peace, and people will return to their homes and live

together side by side with Israelis, and build bridges—not
walls—between us.”

ON JANUARY 30, 2018, the sound of an incoming text wakes
me. Usually I ignore the phone until my alarm sounds, but
for some reason, this time I roll over to check. It's from my
mom to my siblings and me: “We learned on Facebook that
Mr. Awwad has passed.”

I can't believe what I've read. I know Abdullah faced stomach cancer almost a decade ago, but it's long been in remis-
sion, and he seemed healthy and happy when I last saw him.
I need to check the news for myself. I open Facebook and go
to Abdullah's daughter's page. The first post I see is a friend
of the family offering condolences on the passing of Abdullah.

My wife, Brittany, is in front of the bathroom mirror getting ready for work. She hears the sound of my weeping, and
bursts through the door.

“Michael! What's wrong?” I'm sure by the sound of my
cries she thinks someone in the family is dead.

I can barely choke out the terrible truth. “Abdullah died.”
With a face full of compassion, she holds me while I cry. Someone in the family *has* died.

I'm unable to travel to Palestine for the funeral a few days
later. I remember and grieve him from across the world. I soon
learn that for the days and weeks before his sudden death,
Abdullah did not want to leave his home in Beit Sahour. The
morning he passed, his son-in-law had come to take Abdullah
north to Ramallah for a health visit. They walked together out
his front door and into the carport at the edge of the property.
But that was all Abdullah could do, or maybe all he would do.
He collapsed there, in the driveway, and died.

I can't help but find that unbearably poetic. "Welcome to my paradise!" Abdullah always exclaimed. He would say, "I am like a fish. Take a fish out of water, it dies. Take me from my paradise, and I will be like the fish. Believe me, if I die in my paradise, I would die with a smile on my face." I can't count how many times he would tell me how he preferred the humble rocks of his Palestinian paradise to even the soaring Alps of Switzerland. His soul was in the soil, he'd say, in the grape trees, the figs, and the lemons.

And there, at the very end of it all, Abdullah's body couldn't leave. It walked to the outer edges of his home but no farther; it would not cross the threshold. He fell—lost himself to his home, took his final breath in the rich air of his garden.

I guess he couldn't bear to leave. Fortunately, it was paradise.

6

PLACE OF LUMPY CROSSINGS

I once asked a woman here in Belfast to help me understand what it was like growing up here during the Troubles. The Troubles were a multidecade violent conflict that killed more than thirty-five hundred people, mostly where I am now in the northern part of the island of Ireland. The woman I spoke with remembered when she was a child and a loud noise boomed in the distance one night. It scared her, and so she cried for her mother. "My mum walks in to assure me everything's all right," she told me. "And Mum says, 'Don't fret, dear. It wasn't thunder. It was just a bomb.'"

THE SUN BEAT DOWN in full view when I left Israel. As I step off the plane onto the tarmac at Belfast City Airport, it's raining. Of course. It's little wonder this Emerald Isle is so green; it's always wet. I don't love rainy days, yet I love this island.

In particular, I love the northern part of the island. And in the north, it's this Antrim Coast I love most.

I lived here in Belfast during graduate school in the 2012–13 academic year, studying conflict resolution and reconciliation. Something awakened in me then that was always meant to be awake. Sometimes I feel as if I were born in the United States by mistake, that I should have been born in Ireland. But my Irish ancestors landed on the eastern shores of the United States more than two hundred years ago, so that ship literally sailed a long way back. Still, the first time I stepped foot here, it felt like a homecoming.

I am struck this time by the transition from Israel and Palestine. Both here and there are home to complicated conflicts. Both conflicts have to do with land, colonialism, identities, messy histories, belonging, bereavement, and a misuse of religion. There isn't consensus over any of that, though. If you put ten people in a room in either place, you'll hear eleven different stories of what the conflict is about. My friend Pádraig Ó Tuama, who lives here, says, "There is conflict about the conflict."

There is also conflict over language, particularly about what to call "here." In Israel and Palestine, "here" is called by many names depending on your politics: Israel, Palestine, West Bank and Gaza, occupied territories, administered territories, Judea and Samaria—and the list goes on. The same is true on this island.

On my return to Belfast during my first round trip by train to Dublin during grad school, I sat across from a white-haired woman with a soft smile. She asked as we approached Belfast, "And how have you found being in our country?"

"Well, I haven't been long in Northern Ireland, but I've loved what I've experienced so far," I said.

"Oh. Well, dear," she began, tilting her head and lifting her brow, "we call it 'the north of Ireland.'"

I learned then that you have to learn quickly here.

For some, like my language-corrector on the train that day, this whole island is Ireland, and where I am now, in Belfast, is just the northern part of it. For others, this northern part of Ireland is called Northern Ireland, and the separateness matters. They say Northern Ireland is absolutely *not* part of Ireland; it is part of the United Kingdom. Some here identify as British, others as Irish, others as Northern Irish, and still others as perhaps some of all. There is no way to talk about either place without revealing bias or ignorance.

For me, I find myself stumbling toward a tendency to call this place the north of Ireland. I know people here, though, who would say that I just erased their homeland with that language. There is no easy language for here. For now, I'll call it northern Ireland, with a small *n*: a nod toward those who see the region as separate from Ireland, and a nod toward those who see that separation as a false dichotomy. It's not uncomplicated, but it will have to do for now.[1]

THERE'S A THEORY IN PEACEBUILDING that it can take as long to heal from a conflict as the conflict itself lasted.[2] In twelve-step recovery circles, they say that if you go twenty miles into the woods, it's twenty miles back out. Depending on whom you ask, the conflict in northern Ireland lasted eight hundred years, four hundred years, or thirty years. The Good Friday

1. I first saw "northern Ireland" used by a friend of mine from Belfast named Gareth Higgins. His work is worth looking into at www.GarethHiggins.net.
2. I first encountered this idea in John Paul Lederach, "Five Qualities of Practice in Support of Reconciliation Processes," in *Forgiveness and Reconciliation: Religion, Public Policy, and Conflict Transformation*, ed. Raymond G. Helmick and Rodney L. Petersen (Philadelphia: Templeton Foundation Press, 2001), 202.

Agreement (aka the Belfast Agreement) officially ended the long period of violence as recently as 1998. So any way you spin it, this place isn't very far along the healing journey.

The violence here lasted so long, in fact, that it became almost normal. In my last taxi ride during grad school, the driver picked me up on the Antrim Road to carry me down to city center, where I was meeting classmates for a parting glass.

"Do you like living here?" I asked.

He didn't hesitate. "I liked it better in the good old days—twenty to thirty years ago."

I knew from my study of the Troubles that those were not good years in Belfast; in fact, they were some of the worst.

"Why were you happier then? It was a pretty violent time, right?"

"It weren't that violent, so it weren't," he said, glancing at me in the rearview mirror. "It were a pretty stable time, other than the bombs and guns and murders."

Right, I thought; other than those. I asked him if he'd been affected much by the violence.

"No, not too much," he said without any thought. "I mean, there was the time I saw my brother walking down the Falls Road, and a black taxi pulled up, rolled down its window, and blew his head off. I remember seeing my mother trying to put his brains back in."

There was silence. I sat back in my seat as if pulled by a weight, unsettled by both the story and the measured way he told it. He spoke as if it were not unusual, as if it almost were not noteworthy, as if it were not seismic.

A few minutes after he finished his story, we arrived at the pub. I tipped him and thanked him for the conversation. Then I watched as he drove off, down streets that once held the blood of people like his brother.

PEACEBUILDING THEORY has a word for us in the United States too. I can't count how many times I've heard something like, "Slavery was a few hundred years ago. Can we stop talking about it all the time?" Or, "Black people have had equal rights for more than fifty years. Obama was president, after all. Race wouldn't be an issue if we didn't talk about it so much."

It strikes me as important to remember, first of all, that the abomination of slavery is not ancient history. Chattel slavery ended just over a hundred and fifty years ago. Then it morphed into convict leasing. And today, slavery has a new manifestation in the violence of mass incarceration. Even the famous Thirteenth Amendment of the U.S. Constitution allows for this, stating that slavery and involuntary servitude are forbidden *except* as punishment for a convicted crime. In between all that, more than four thousand black Americans were lynched by white terrorists—which is really important language to use here. And Jim Crow laws stunted the lives and stole the liberties of millions of black citizens.[3]

But we in the United States know this. If we pause long enough to think rather than just react, we know when chattel slavery ended. We know that millions of black and brown humans were abducted, brutalized, bereaved, and forced to labor for free for generations upon generations upon generations so that the people who thought they were "white" could make a profit.[4] We know that white people chased, captured, beat, burned, mutilated, and murdered black people in

---

3. For more on this, see Michelle Alexander, *The New Jim Crow* (New York: The New Press, 2012); and Equal Justice Initiative, *Lynching in America: Confronting the Legacy of Racial Terror*, 3rd ed. (Montgomery, AL, Equal Justice Initiative, 2017), https://lynchinginamerica.eji.org/report/. I also highly recommend director Ava DuVernay's Oscar-nominated documentary *13th* (Los Angeles: Kandoo Films, 2016), currently available on Netflix.

4. I was first introduced to the language of people thinking they are white in Ta-Nehisi Coates's brilliant book *Between the World and Me* (New York: Spiegel and Grau, 2015).

lynchings and other forms of terror. We know that Jim Crow was alive and well in our own, our parents', or our grandparents' lifetimes. We know how recent it was.

What we must learn is that it can take as long to get out of a conflict as it took to get in it. For simplicity's sake, if we chart the duration of this "conflict" of racism only from the arrival in North America of the first kidnapped Africans to the signing of the Civil Rights Act (though of course this did not actually end the scourge of racism), we can start in 1619 and drag the timeline through the centuries to 1964. That's a period of 345 years. If we were in a "post-conflict" healing journey, then we'd be only fifty years or so into a *very* long process. To say that race should now be a nonissue in America is to reveal a profound ignorance about the nature of conflict and reconciliation. We aren't out of the woods yet. Not by a long shot.

But rather than let this lead to despair, we'd be wise to let it lead to courage, hope, and action. We get to be *part* of the journey toward healing and transforming our fractured communities. None of us need to be saviors; we just need to contribute. Extraordinary and ordinary contributions—they all belong.

OVER THE YEARS here in northern Ireland, various places have emerged as sites of healing and harbor. One of the most consistent is Corrymeela, where I am now. Corrymeela is on the northern coast near Ballycastle, a village that fits every image in your mind of a quaint Irish town. Corrymeela is both a network of people and a particular place. It's a physical refuge fifty miles outside Belfast where people fled for safety during the Troubles, a refuge that is a long-standing witness to hope

in the midst of violence. Today, it still thrives as a center teem-
ing with life thanks to a dedicated staff, rotating volunteer
cohorts, and a full calendar of events addressing issues of
sectarianism, marginalization, legacies of conflict, and public
theology.[5]

The Corrymeela Ballycastle Centre sits on a gorgeous green
cliff facing north toward Rathlin Island and the Scottish isles.
A black road leads down the hillside toward Ballycastle. The
road is so narrow you could hop across it if you tried hard,
yet somehow the locals manage to operate two lanes of traffic
on it. I love walking this road. It winds and weaves between
the hillsides and rocky coast so drastically you can rarely
see more than one hundred feet of road ahead of you. Wild
blackberries, daisies, red and purple flowers, and long grasses
decorate the edges of the road. Along the coastline, seabirds
sweep across the face of the water, darting into the waves to
hunt for food. When I'm back home, remembering this place,
I can still feel the brisk breeze on my face and hear the call of
the birds across the air.

Throughout the decades, Corrymeela has offered a place
for people to transform division through encountering one
another. More than ten thousand people a year, of all ages,
come through the center. The community is committed to the
project of learning how to live well together, especially among
difference. This is what reconciliation is about: learning to
live together well. Corrymeela has welcomed Protestants and
Catholics, Loyalists and Republicans,[6] victims and combatants, and political leaders and peacemakers the world over.

---

5. For more information about the Corrymeela Community, see www.corrymeela.org.
6. The term *Republican* here has no correlation to the term *Republican* in the U.S.
   context. In simplified terms, Republicans in northern Ireland support the creation of
   a united Ireland, joining the northern counties with the southern Republic of Ireland.
   Loyalists are people loyal to the United Kingdom, who wish for northern Ireland to
   remain officially part of the UK.

Over cups of tea, beside warm fireplaces, and through difficult and daring dialogue, healing happens here.

When I ask my friend Pádraig, the leader of Corrymeela—to whom I go for all Irish questions—what the name Corrymeela means, he tells me this story. Some time ago, people gave that name to the land where the center sits. They thought it meant "hill of harmony" in Old Irish. And what a lovely name, they thought, for a place of reconciliation: hill of harmony.

Years later, someone came along who actually knew what they were talking about when it came to Old Irish etymology and said, "Actually, *corrymeela* means something more like 'place of lumpy crossings.'" And all the people breathed a sigh of relief. In their work for reconciliation, harmony had been hard to come by. But "place of lumpy crossings"? That was a name they could claim with integrity.[7]

I love this story. It's inviting and liberating. Corrymeela has taught me that the work of reconciliation rarely looks lovely and sweet. Antagonistic people are not often found arm in arm, watching the sunset, singing of common ground and friendship. Rather, the journey of reconciliation might look more like Strider and the hobbits, J. R. R. Tolkien's beloved characters, trudging through the bogs toward Rivendell. Stumbling over the lumpy earth, trying to cross on grassy mounds but slipping into knee-deep muck. That's the road of reconciliation. It's hard. And it hurts.

The only people who say that reconciliation is easy are people who have never done it. If reconciling across deep division were easy, it wouldn't re-traumatize people. If facilitating courageous conversations were easy, we wouldn't need trained facilitators and counselors. If transforming conflict were easy, more people would do it well. Trying to walk with others in

---

7. Pádraig is no longer leader of Corrymeela. He left that position in April 2019.

the place of "lumpy crossings" is to bear witness to pain. It's to see people at their most vulnerable. Filled with fear and still leaning into courage. It is to look upon human frailty and failure, and to see simultaneously resiliency and resurrection.

Corrymeela has taught me that this work does not require that enemies find consensus or common ground on every issue dividing them. What *is* needed is a willingness to understand, which is no small feat. To say it can be difficult to sit in the room with someone whose ideology we find incomprehensible is an understatement. Sometimes it feels impossible. Torturous. Unbearable. Sometimes, these people even threaten our sense of self and safety. Staying in the room and trying to understand the perspectives we consider indefensible can feel wrong, because listening and learning may seem like complicity.

Once when I was here at Corrymeela, I heard Pádraig speak about this in the context of the politics of this place. Protestants and Catholics at times struggle to stay in the same room with each other. Listening to understand can lead others to think you're agreeing with them. And we don't want to look complicit when it comes to the perspective of our enemies; we want to look resolute in our disdain. Pádraig explained, however, that understanding is not complicity; understanding is just understanding.

Being able to articulate the story of the other is an indispensable skill in transforming conflict into something that can help us. If we cannot summarize the other's position in a way that feels recognizable to them, we probably don't understand. Understanding their belief is not the same as justifying it, or agreeing with it, or supporting it. It's simply being able to get your head around how that person, with their story and their pain and their experiences and their relationships and their wiring, might come to think and act as they do.

It's curious how much we can resist understanding perspectives we don't agree with. Maybe we're nervous we'll be converted—because being converted to new thinking can be dangerous. We build whole worlds around certain ways of thinking. To risk conversion is to risk the unmaking of those worlds. And sometimes it's easier to believe a lie than to chance being unraveled by a truth.

Pádraig says that "peace is holding deeply dividing tensions but continuing in a democratic process." Any citizen of a democracy can tell you that democracies are filled with conflict, violence, and division. Where two or more are gathered, there will be conflict. It's just part of living. Sometimes the best path forward may not be searching for common ground but rather learning to live well together on the ground that we're currently on.

In facilitating storytelling circles, I often hear people say things like, "This experience reminds me how much we all have in common. Most of the time, we're focused on our differences, but we just need to remember that we are more alike than we are different." This is an important—even transformative—sentiment. It certainly helps to learn how those we fear are actually like us. At the same time, though, prioritizing the search for common ground also runs the risk of assuming difference is bad. That it must be overcome. We tend to see difference as a dangerous enemy. But perhaps we can come to see difference as a complicated friend.

I'm cautious to believe common ground will be what saves us—because there may not always be enough of it. What *might* save us is learning how to live well with difference. Corrymeela has witnessed to this truth for more than fifty years. We will never live among people exactly like us. What will always be true for people living next to other people is that we will differ, in large and small ways. Where common ground can remind us of shared humanity, we should embrace it. And where it can't, we should remember that uncommon ground is not evidence of unshared humanity.

IN MANY WAYS, northern Ireland reminds me of home. Some of these ways are lovely expressions of culture and goodness. In Nashville, and particularly when I return to my childhood roots in rural East Tennessee, the similarities in language, food, music, and values are difficult to ignore. For instance, my maternal family line has lived in middle Tennessee since the mid-1800s, after our ancestors from Ireland and the British Isles landed in Virginia. Growing up, I wondered about some of the expressions I heard from that side of that family. In particular, my mom's brother Steve, who in response to a simple "Hey, Steve," routinely replies, "How 'bout it?" Not until I lived in Belfast did this make sense. I entered a room and my classmate John, a middle-aged local guy, greeted me with, "How 'bout ye there, Michael?" And it clicked—whether consciously or not, Steve was speaking from his ancestral roots. I was elated, and called home immediately to tell my mother.

At the moment, though, as I'm considering the connections between here and home, I'm thinking of segregation and suspicion. As I noted earlier, there's an expression in Belfast: "Whatever you say, say nothing." People in the northern part of the island speak this phrase as a caution. After decades of mayhem and murder by people who look alike, it can be hard to know whom to trust, so discretion proves prudent.

To discern if the person they're speaking with is "one of us or one of them," folks ask questions that appear innocent enough on the surface. "What's your name?" "Where are you from?" And then they listen hard. Is your name Catholic or Protestant? Do you live on a Catholic street or a Protestant one? Is your accent one of "ours" or one of "theirs"? Particularly twenty, thirty, or forty years ago, if you gave the wrong answer to any of those questions, you might end up dead.

In times of conflict, people often huddle with those who share a single, unifying denominator: Catholic, Protestant, white, black, Republican, Democrat. We need uncomplicated markings to reduce our chance of danger. In northern Ireland, these markings most often fall along the sectarian lines of Protestant and Catholic. And extending from those, political and national lines as well—Irish or British? Loyalist or Republican? If you know how to identify a person, you know whether to assume they're safe or unsafe.

We do the same thing in the United States. We have similar sectarian fears but with different names, like Islamophobia and anti-Semitism, to name a couple. Too many of us draw hard boundaries around identifiers like race, country of origin, politics, and gender. And we have our own investigative questions. "Where are you really from?" white folks might ask a person of color if the first answer to the question wasn't foreign enough. Consistent with growing patterns worldwide, many Americans have become deeply suspicious of anyone "foreign"—specifically, anyone whose skin is darker than their own. We'd be wise to acknowledge that racism is the underpinning of our xenophobia, and how we reward those who champion our racist suspicion. The very person who fueled the obsession with President Obama's faith and place of birth was then elected the next president.

In my grad school days in Belfast, one of my professors assigned the insightful and thorough book *Moving beyond Sectarianism*, by Joseph Liechty and Cecilia Clegg. Focused on the northern Irish context, the authors chart an eleven-point "scale of sectarian danger." These eleven statements represent measurements for acknowledging and assessing difference.

1. We are different, we believe differently.
2. We are right.
3. We are right and you are wrong.
4. You are a less adequate version of what we are.
5. You are not what you say you are.
6. We are in fact what you say you are.
7. What you are doing is evil.
8. You are so wrong that you forfeit ordinary rights.
9. You are less than human.
10. You are evil.
11. You are demonic.[8]

Some of these can be necessary and reasonable statements—like statements 1, 2, 3, and 7. Naming difference does not need to be dangerous. Believing in one's moral or intellectual correctness is natural and can still leave room for another's right to hold different perspectives, even if we disagree. And calling out evil is a moral obligation. Other statements on this scale, though—like 8, 9, 10, and 11—are ripe with violent potential. These statements infect too much of the politics in the United States. We deploy such rhetoric and thought with lightning speed, often through our scapegoating.

Scapegoating distracts us from the kind of deep examination and diagnosis that could lead to radical healing and change. Almost always, the problems we face—socially or individually—are multifaceted. Scapegoating leads us to believe our problems are simple and therefore have simple solutions. This

---

8. Joseph Liechty and Cecilia Clegg, *Moving beyond Sectarianism: Religion, Conflict, and Reconciliation in Northern Ireland* (Dublin: The Columba Press, 2001), 245.

does not produce the kind of diagnosis that facilitates sustainable change.

We lie to ourselves if we say nothing in this world is actually perpetuating evil. Sometimes there *are* villains. Sometimes we need to say, "You are wrong, and what you are doing is evil." But when we allow those necessary statements to morph into "You are evil, demonic, less than human, and undeserving of the same rights I am worthy of," we become accomplices to and perpetrators of violence.

I know this may seem dismal, but these reflections are the stuff of hope to me. If we ever want to march out of the hell of our divisions, we must tell the truth about ourselves. We need to become aware of the ways in which we're moving further along the "scale of sectarian danger." We need to hold each other accountable for our violent scapegoating, dehumanizing, and marginalizing. Ignoring the larger problematic narratives while exalting feel-good anecdotes helps no one. But coming face-to-face with the world—as it is and as *we* are—using simple and true language for what we see and refusing to turn away: this can help us. Then the stories of hope we tell have weight. They point us toward the light even while we remain fully aware of the darkness surrounding us.

After more than three hundred pages of diagnosing the problem of sectarianism in northern Ireland, Liechty and Clegg offer some steps for moving beyond it:

1. Maintain a clear and steady vision that all people are implicated in the system and that every level and structure of society is tainted by sectarianism, however indirectly.
2. Maintain a consistent and clear commitment to act in order to challenge sectarianism.

3. Name and expose sectarian dynamics, action, attitudes, beliefs, and structures wherever they are recognized.

4. Take risks to break the cycle of antagonized division.

5. Develop a vision of reconciled community in Northern Ireland.[9]

These five practices are as relevant for people of peace, justice, and goodwill in the United States as they are for the people of northern Ireland. Whether we consider our own sectarianism, racism, anti-Semitism, Islamophobia, sexism, xenophobia, homophobia, transphobia, or any other prejudice or oppression, we need to adopt this wisdom. It will be part of what saves us.

ON THE NORTHEAST CLIFF of Corrymeela, above the Drumaroan Road, a bench rests beside a sturdy wooden cross. Both face the choppy waters of the North Channel. I come here to sit, often with a steaming cup of tea, peering out to the blue horizon where the Irish Sea meets the Atlantic. It's here I reflect on the learning of this place, with lessons as many as the waves below. Corrymeela is part of what helps me see more wisely.

This safe haven teaches me that we all need shelter and sanctuary in times of conflict. Seeking refuge isn't always permanent escape. Sometimes our survival depends on leaving, and the refuge may be what allows us to *return* to the sites of pain rather than abandon them.

Corrymeela teaches me that we need spaces to encounter each other on equitable footing. For productive dialogue to have a chance, we may need to step away from the charged places of our daily lives and conflicts and find another place,

---

9. Ibid., 343.

on neutral turf, where the issues dividing us can be addressed without the trauma of our homeplaces overcoming us.

Corrymeela teaches me that we can't be defined by victimhood forever. There are times when owning our victimization is necessary, when it is damning to those wielding violent power, when it can be part of what leads us toward liberation. And then there are times to let that identity go because clinging to it will only bring us back to violence.

Corrymeela teaches me that proximity is essential, but it's not a panacea. Uncritical articulations of reconciliation suggest that if people just meet one another, they won't be able to hate each other. This is called the "contact hypothesis": the idea that getting proximate is the cure. But this is too limited. For most of human history, you couldn't kill someone until you got close to them. Wars, prisons, and slave plantations alone are sufficient proof that meeting one another doesn't necessarily lead to peace. Sometimes, proximity may lead to deeper violence. As Corrymeela's former executive director Colin Craig said to me recently, "Sometimes, sitting with the other and hearing their story may make you say, 'Yes, now I remember *exactly* why I want to kill you.'" Corrymeela teaches me that without values and practices like curiosity and humility, proximity may just get you within firing range.[10]

Corrymeela teaches me that the stories we grow up with may not be the ones we need to keep. To reach for peace, we must let go of our weapons, including the ones known as narratives.

---

10. For much more on this, see Michael T. McRay, "How to Dismantle an Enemy," in *Voices of Freedom from Asia and the Middle East*, ed. Rima Abunasser and Mark Dennis (Albany, NY: SUNY Press, forthcoming).

Corrymeela teaches me that if we do not live with courage, from the heart, then our dreams of peace will slip through our fingers like the sand on the shore below.

Corrymeela teaches me that the path of reconciliation is one of lumpy crossings. It is filled with obstacles and dead ends and unexpected holes. It requires muscular, exhausting commitments to justice, empathy, openness, compromise, and sacrifice. Corrymeela teaches me that reconciliation will likely look less like harmony and more like honest struggle to do all we can to live together without violence. And sometimes, that will have to be enough.

7

I'VE JUST MET THE ENEMY

Jo Berry was only twenty-seven years old when the Irish Republican Army killed her father. On October 12, 1984, a bomb went off at the Grand Hotel in Brighton, England, where Britain's Conservative Party was hosting its annual conference. Jo's sister called her to say a bomb had detonated at the hotel where their father and stepmother were staying. Jo looks at me, takes a breath, and smiles. It's a small smile, almost forced, perhaps to ease the pain of telling the story. She says, "And so that was the beginning of waiting, waiting for news. And my brother then went to the hospital in Brighton and found my stepmother injured, but still no news of my dad. And unfortunately, at four in the afternoon, we got news that his body had been identified, and he was dead. And the IRA said they were responsible for it."

Jo's father, Sir Anthony Berry, was a member of parliament (MP) in England. The IRA was a paramilitary group that took up arms to fight against what it called the British occupation of the north of Ireland. British soldiers in northern Ireland, Protestant Loyalist paramilitaries, British-identifying citizens of northern Ireland, and even British government officials were all IRA targets. To some, the IRA was a liberation army. To others, it was a terrorist organization.

Jo is now in her late fifties and happens to be visiting Belfast this week while I'm here. The only day she has free is a day I am up the coast at Corrymeela, and to my delight and surprise, Jo has graciously agreed to travel north to Corrymeela for us to talk. We're speaking together in the orange living room of Cedar Haven, Pádraig's cottage when he's working at the center. Jo is on the sofa, straight-brown hair falling past her shoulders onto her flower-laced blue top. I'm in a chair facing her. A small table rests between us, holding the pot of tea I've just drawn.

Jo tells me that five people died in that bombing. Her father was the only MP.

"Part of me also died in that bomb," she says, "the part of me that had no responsibilities and was living in peacetime, I suppose. So I decided within two days afterwards—I went somewhere in London that meant a lot to me and decided to set intention to make something positive out of this and understand those who killed him. So that was within two days, which was very soon, really. But the reason why I think it was so soon was because I was having to almost start again, and I did believe in peace and actually thought about nonviolence and Gandhi. But losing my father in that attack, in that terrorist attack, was so public—and losing my father in such a violent way, I had to do something really different. And so I decided to go on a journey.

"And at that time, I didn't know anyone else who was on this mad journey of trying to understand who killed their loved one. But I very much trusted life would bring me the experience, and it did. And I ended up maybe three months later sharing a taxi with this stranger in London, and when I was in the taxi, it turned out that he was from Belfast. And I said to him, 'That's a bit of a coincidence, because the IRA just killed my father in a terrorist attack.' And he said, 'My brother was in the IRA. And my brother was killed last year by a British soldier.'"

Jo pauses and looks up from the table to catch my eyes. "And so we should be enemies; we came from different sides. And yet we spoke in that taxi of a world where people didn't go and kill each other and where there was no enemy anymore and dreamt of a vision of a peaceful world. And I remember leaving the taxi and the thought came to me, 'I can build a bridge across the divide. That is one thing I can do to help.' And it seemed that building that bridge was a step in bringing something positive."

To this day, Jo doesn't know the name of the man in the taxi that night, and she's never seen him again. But not long after that, she began traveling to Belfast, where she met people with similar stories of pain and loss.

"I began to hear stories and share," she says, "and it was all part of me beginning to understand why someone would join the IRA. But I hadn't done any emotional work, and so after a few years, I stopped coming. Then, when the Good Friday peace agreement happened, my life changed again."

It's common for peace agreements to include the release of prisoners of war and political prisoners. The 1998 Belfast Agreement was no exception. Political prisoners of the Troubles walked free, including Patrick Magee—the IRA man responsible for the Brighton bombing.

"I remember turning on a TV and seeing him being released from prison," Jo says. "I had no idea it was going to be that day. I kind of thought at some time it might happen. But there he was. And I was quite shocked. I remember thinking, 'It's all right for you. You're free. You know, my dad can never come back.'"

For years, Jo had suppressed the grief and anger and pain. "I didn't have any help," she tells me. "No one offered counseling or said, 'Maybe you need some emotional help.' And I did not know how to deal with such difficult emotions. I just didn't—I had no idea. So I remember pushing them down when the pain got too much. I couldn't cope with the pain, so I pushed it down. And of course, that's not a very healthy thing to do. And it had repercussions, but you try your best at the time. So all these emotions came up one day, and that's when I realized I needed to attend to my own healing."

Jo found herself taking part in a workshop at the Glencree Centre for Peace and Reconciliation in Ireland's Wicklow Mountains. The moment she walked through the door, she knew she'd come to the right place.

"I remember being at Glencree and opening the door, and there was a guy whose son was killed in the Warrington bomb, parents of soldiers killed, someone injured in the Birmingham bombing, and just knowing it was safe for me to open up and share my story. No one's going to say, 'Oh, haven't you let go yet?' You know, they understand. And so I did a lot of sharing that weekend, and the next weekend I went and did a lot of crying and raging and also laughing and connecting. I met people from different sides who'd lost loved ones."

Through these healing experiences, Jo realized she had a desire to meet Patrick, the man who killed her father. All roads had been leading here. Jo discovered that in the Glencree network, several people knew Patrick. They tried to set up a connection, but Patrick refused. Then in December

2000, Jo received a call from a friend in Dublin who said, "I've arranged for Patrick to be in my house this evening. Can you come?"

"Where were you at the time?" I ask Jo.

"I was in North Wales. And I was preparing to go to Glencree for another weekend. And I remember when the phone call came, my first thought was that I'm not in the mood to meet him today. I'm not feeling exciting, inspired, or curious about him. Then I thought, 'No, I'm going to trust this. This is a day I've been wanting to happen. And yes, it's scary and overwhelming, but I want to do this.' So off I went.

"I got the ferry from Holyhead to Dublin and all the time just so scared and not knowing what I was going to say or feel, you know. What would he say? Would I regret it? You know, the mind just going over it all. But I got to Anne's house, and I sat there and I waited. And on the absolute dot of seven thirty, a knock on the door, and he walked in. And I remember I got up from the table and shook his hand and thanked him for coming."

Jo doesn't pause in her story, but I am struck that after all those years of waiting to meet her father's killer, the first words out of her mouth were welcome, and thanks.

"I remember thinking he might not even turn up," she continues. "You know—he could change his mind. So I was really pleased he was there. And he said, 'I really appreciate you asking me to come. Thank you.' And then I went, 'Well, I'm pleased you agreed, because I heard you didn't want to see me.' And then he said, 'Oh no, I've been asked a few times to meet you and I've always said yes.' So we discussed how his yeses got turned into nos, and that kind of broke the ice. And we went into our own room, just the two of us. That first meeting was three hours.

"And, you know, I was really curious. I really wanted him to open up, you know. I didn't want to go there interrogating him or arguing or telling him he was bad. My need was really to hear his story. And so I almost facilitated him to open up. I did share also about my dad and what had happened to me since then, but I also asked him a lot of questions. About half-way through, he'd been giving me a lot of political justification on why it'd been a good strategy to bomb the hotel. I'd heard that before, you know; it wasn't the first time. So I wanted more from him, but I was becoming aware that this could only be one meeting, because I wasn't going to have my dad's death justified in that way. It wouldn't have been good for me. But what I wanted was to see some of his humanity. And I could see from the beginning that he was someone who had sensitivity and thought deeply. Just sort of apparent in how he was. So I got what I wanted out of it, and was thinking, 'I am going to end it soon.' And at that point, he changed. And he stopped talking, and he rubbed his eye and said, 'I don't know anymore what to say. I don't know who I am. I want to hear your anger and your rage. And what can I do to help you?'

"And when that happened, I remember part of me just wanted to leave the room as quickly as possible, because this was much more than I'd bargained for. And part of me really welcomed this as a start of something different. And it was him taking off the political hat and opening up. And what had been just about my need now became *his* need. It was the beginning of him seeing that he'd lost some of his humanity in a way which he didn't know he had done before, and him really wanting to hear more about the effects on me.

"And so the conversation was really different after that. After about an hour and a half, I couldn't sustain anymore. I had a voice in my head going, 'What are you doing sitting here? He killed your father. You shouldn't be doing this.' There was a lot going on in me, and I wanted to be present to him. But I got to the point where I thought, 'I actually can't sustain this anymore.' And now I knew it wasn't the end. We were going to meet again. I knew it wasn't finished."

Later on, Jo got in touch with Patrick again, ready for their next conversation. And to her surprise, he apologized. "He said he was really sorry that he killed my dad. And he said it with great feeling, and I said to him, 'I'm so glad it's you.' And he didn't know what that meant, and nor did I, but what I meant was his preparedness to open up. And he would later say that if I'd gone in arguing, going, 'I'm right and you're wrong,' he would just stay in a very safe place of righteousness."

Jo takes a moment, recollecting. "He later said that he was disarmed by the fact that I gave him empathy. And that was much harder for him—to receive my empathy. And that sort of changed him, so then he started his own journey. And I know after that, we both felt, you know, very disoriented. I remember going back to where I lived and being almost just broken thinking that I've just met the enemy, and I've seen his humanity. Where does that leave me?"

IN THE GOSPEL OF MATTHEW, Jesus tells his disciples a story about the day of judgment. He says he will separate and judge those gathered before him on the basis of how they treated "the least of these." The most vulnerable. The undesirable. The suspicious. The people on the margins. Jesus said the judged will be told that whenever they fed the hungry, welcomed the stranger, clothed the naked, and visited the prisoner, they were actually doing those things for him. He was telling them that when he's gone, they will find him as and among "the least of these."

I've always been struck that Jesus seems to *assume* his followers will be with such people and in such places. Like prison. Jesus apparently thinks it's a given that his disciples will visit prisoners. Being a Christian myself, I decided I probably should get to it. So in the middle of my junior year of college at Lipscomb University, I began regular visits to Riverbend Maximum Security Institution in Nashville.

I've never met an enemy. I'm not sure I even have one. Certainly not like Jo. And so the closest I've ever come to such a meeting was stepping foot inside Riverbend prison for the first time. I have loved ones who've been raped. I love people who've had loved ones murdered. To meet incarcerated men who had perpetuated such harm was jarring. Whenever I laughed in that first visit, I remember a voice in my head asking, "Would you be acting this way if one of their victims were in the room?" And the answer is, of course not. But I also realized that didn't mean that my presence or laughter was inappropriate.

Like Jo, I shook hands with these men, thanked them for welcoming me into their space, and sat around a table talking for two hours. It was a deeply confusing experience. I knew of the horrible violence they had committed, and I also was learning of their kindness, humor, faith, friendships, compassion, and stories. In short, I was seeing their humanity, and I exited the prison checkpoint that first night unsure of how I felt. All I knew was that would not be our only meeting.

I suppose I'm trying to connect Jo's experience to something in my own life, though I know this comparison falls short. Still, I'm wondering if, in some small way, I understand a bit of what she felt after meeting Patrick. I'd like to hear more about what she was thinking when he walked through the door and she thanked him for coming. So I ask her why she greeted him that way.

"Because I really saw it as a courageous thing to turn up when many wouldn't. And the years of work I'd done on myself had led me to the point where I could almost see what he did as *separate* from himself. I wanted to rehumanize him; I didn't want to demonize him. I didn't see him as an evil person for doing that; I saw him as someone who, like all of us, had been born wanting. He had ambitions in his life and got caught up in violence. Yes, he *chose* to use violence, but that didn't mean he was a bad person. It was a bad thing to do."

I ask Jo whether this way of engaging Patrick—rehumanizing him, separating the personhood from the action—was natural for her. Was it instinctive, or did she need to cultivate that?

"No, I'd worked on that," she says, nodding several times. "My wish to not blame, to not make him responsible for my pain, was the beginning. I had no control that he killed my father. I *could* control my choice of how I felt afterwards. So it was about taking responsibility for my feelings so I could then transform them. If I'd made him responsible, I could have never transformed them. And so that relationship with him was straightaway, even though I didn't even have a name. And to me it had to be healed, because I *did* have an enemy. He *did* kill my father."

DURING THE SIXTEEN YEARS between her father's murder and meeting Patrick, Jo was getting herself ready. She was working, with intention, on her interior life. Too often, people passionate about "bridge work," like myself, jump to the *bridging* part of the work. We tend to skip over or rush through the necessary foundation laying.

Once, someone contacted me about working with him to facilitate a storytelling circle process between police and incarcerated youth in his town. He was connected with the police department, and he saw a need for this bridging work. But in our few initial conversations, he offered no plan for building trust with the vulnerable youth in juvenile detention. He wanted to go straight to the bridging part, planning the experience when the cops and kids would sit in a circle together and listen to each other's stories.

We are putting the cart ahead of the horse, I told him; let's slow down. At the very least, I said, we need a long-term plan, key objectives, a risk-benefit analysis, and confidence that the youth can have agency in the process and can give informed consent. We also needed a commitment to "single identity work," a phrase I encountered through studying peacebuilding. It refers to the importance of working with individual groups separately before facilitating a meeting between them. Let's facilitate some story processes with the youth by themselves, I told him. No outsiders. We'll do the same within the police. Let each group build trust and familiarity and comfort with the process *before* asking them to reach across the divide.

When my friend Salim Munayer takes Palestinian and Israeli youth into the Negev Desert for relationship building through his organization Musalaha, he does his due diligence, working first with the Palestinian kids on their own and the Israeli kids on their own. The meeting comes later. Peacebuilder John Paul Lederach puts it this way, "You do not build a bridge starting in the middle. You start with a strong foundation on each shore, build toward the middle. When it is solid, others can walk across it."[1]

---

1. John Paul Lederach, "Five Qualities of Practice in Support of Reconciliation Processes," in *Forgiveness and Reconciliation: Religion, Public Policy, and Conflict Transformation*, ed. Raymond G. Helmick and Rodney L. Petersen (Philadelphia: Templeton Foundation Press, 2001), 196.

Jo Berry knew this too, perhaps not even consciously. Her knowledge of this may have been embodied rather than intellectual. But she knew she needed to establish a strong foundation on her shore before she tried to meet Patrick on the bridge. She could not start in the middle; she had to start where she could start: with herself.

I SAY TO JO, "I want to hear, if you would be willing to share, about the process of anger and raging when it comes to grief."

"Yeah, I have raged," she says. "I think every emotion is understandable when you've lost a family member to murder or terrorism or war. It's absolutely understandable, and everyone has their own way of going through the emotions. And it's not helpful to tell someone that anger is bad. Anger is a really important emotion—and rage too. And to me, the question is how to feel it without hurting another human being."

Jo stops talking for a moment before saying, "I've had a lot of help and support. And the other thing that's really important to me to go with the emotions is the story in my head. I'll give you an example of that. I've had some secondary trauma, which is really common in this situation. Some bad decisions I've made, which again is all understandable. But then, I can get into thinking, because I'm feeling the anger and the pain, and I can go, 'Well, it's all the fault of Patrick. If he hadn't planted a bomb, this wouldn't have happened.' Well, that's a very helpful story in one way, but it's going to keep me in pain. So I also work with the story in my head. I don't want to be a victim. I don't want to see him as a perpetrator. So I work on changing that story, so that it will be, 'I am doing okay. I have the resources I need to overcome this.' Or, 'What do I need right now?' That's a really good question. When I'm really emotionally kaput, what do I need? A hug? Do I need to ring someone? What do I need? You know, it takes it back to myself. It's really interesting—the stories we tell in our head affect our emotions."

Speaking of stories, I want to know the rest of hers. What happened after that first meeting?

"Well, we then met two weeks later," she says, "and some-one came to film it. Purely for a reconciliation group in Belfast. But it turned out to be a documentary. So we went 'public.' That was a big, big step for us both. And very scary, I have to tell you. After the program went out, we got a lot of very pos-itive feedback, which I was really pleased about. Then people started asking us to come speak in different places.

"I remember the first time we spoke was in London, and we were given like five minutes each or something crazy. And I remember Pat said, 'I now know I could sit down and have a cup of tea with Jo's dad. And I didn't know that.' To me, I keep those words. They're very profound. To me, that's what it's all about. He demonized my dad—and *he* would say that. And the Conservative Party [in the UK] demonized the IRA. And that's what goes on in conflict. But I could see the two of them together now. It was very healing. It's not that the Conservative Party were having cups of tea with the IRA, but the fact that he said it and that I could *see* it, it was almost like my dad has come back. Pat *rehumanized* him."

From there, the speaking invitations continued to pile up. Jo and Pat could see the positive effect their stories had on those gathered, and so they kept going. Jo says that since 2001, they've spoken together over 150 times all around the world: Israel, Palestine, Spain and the Basque Country, Rwanda, Leb-anon, Bosnia, across Europe, and more.

In all this travel together, she had a complex epiphany: "I've been to places where he's the only person I know. We give each other support. I care about him. I get frustrated by him, but I do care about him." She hesitates in a kind of dramatic pause before stating her ultimate realization. "He is my friend."

I feel the complexity just hearing her say it. The man who murdered her father is now her friend. Not a colleague to tolerate in order to do important work. A friend.

"It's an unusual friendship," she says. "It really is unusual. Because we're reminded all the time of why we're together. But there are times when we're sitting on planes and he's doing his crossword and trying to teach me how to do a cryptic crossword, you know. It's just normal. And then other times we're, like, *really* in it, having really hard conversations. But since we met, we've had shared experiences together, so he's not just the man who killed my father—"

"He's also the man who teaches you cryptic crossword puzzles," I say.

"Yes," she says with a smile and laugh. "And I'm really bad at them."

JO'S STORY AND HER CAPACITY for compassion reminds me of something an Israeli named Jean Marc said to me not long ago. He explained that in Hebrew and Arabic, the etymological roots of the words *compassion* and *womb* are the same. He said that just as the womb is the body's way of making space for a child, so compassion is creating space inside ourselves for another—for another's stories, identities, and feelings.

I've never been and never will be pregnant, but I can recognize that wombs, while often loving spaces of nurture and joy, are also spaces of pain. I think this is what Jo is describing. The relationship she and Pat have built is not one of naïve, romantic euphoria, but rather is grounded in this womb-like pain of compassion. From just a few days after her father's murder, Jo knew she needed to make something positive of such tragedy, and she set out to understand those responsible for his death. In a similar way, Pat found in that initial conversation with Jo a desire to open himself up to her pain and story. He was disarmed by her empathy, she said. Her compassion begat compassion.

Jo tells me she still challenges Pat and gets angry with him. Sometimes, the pain comes back. To feel compassion for another is to find resonance in that person's experience, to try to situate yourself inside their story. This experience can be agonizing, especially in conflict, as it means surrendering the moral high ground. It means accepting that one's own narrative may not be the only one; there may actually be multiple truths. Compassion requires releasing claims of righteousness, superiority, and victimhood. It means admitting, perhaps for the first time, that the other is fully human too.

"I'M COMPLETELY COMMITTED to peace," Jo says, "and peace is about moving from where we have *the enemy* to actually seeing that there is no *other*. Because what I've learned is that when I really listen to Pat's story and empathize, then I get to the point of thinking, 'Would I have done the same thing if I had lived his life?' And I really don't know. I do know that I don't believe in the concept of *the other* anymore. I believe we're all wounded humans struggling with our circumstances and what happens to us."

At this point, I have told Jo three times that I only have one more question. I'm finding it difficult to wrap up this conversation. She smiles as I tell her again I have only one more question.

"In developing what you've named as a friendship now with Pat," I begin, "how essential was his sense of remorse, or the words 'I'm sorry'? Were those important to hear?"

"I think the most important thing was him acknowledging that he demonized my dad and that now he sees him as a wonderful human being. That's the most important thing. And to me, that is the height of restorative justice. That is what it seeks to do. And that justice means more to me than a normal kind of prison sentence or punitive justice. The justice for me is that he now lives with that—that he knows he killed a wonderful human being. And that feels right to me. And that feels like . . . like—"

"Like justice," I say.

"Yes," she says. "That is justice. That is the best that could come out of this."

I can't resist the urge to keep going. "I guess then this will be the last thing I ask you."

"You obviously can't count," Jo says with a laugh.

I ask Jo about the components of reconciliation, as she's experienced them. What are they? What does reconciliation need? She tells me that, beyond empathy, it needs to happen slowly, in small steps. It needs trust. It needs curiosity and respect for the other's story. It needs self-awareness. It needs to grant each the right to their autonomy, to their own journey. And it needs commitment. Sometimes, we have to withdraw from the process and the relationship to care for ourselves. But in reconciliation, the withdrawal isn't the final word. We have to go back. We have to stay in it.

JO SIPS THE LAST BIT of her tea, setting the mug down as she swallows. It and our conversation are finished. She stands as I turn off the camera. We exchange expressions of gratitude, and I hurry ahead of her to open the door. A slight drizzle moistens our clothes as we step outside. I shake her hand and smile before she walks across the pebble garden toward her car.

Popping back inside, I lift my jacket from the back of the chair, latch the front door behind me, and wade through the tall grasses toward the Croí. *Croí* is the Irish word for "heart," and it is the name Corrymeela has given to its gorgeous stone chapel in the center of the community. At the moment, it's empty of people. In the center of the small chapel is a round wooden table, encircled by two dozen overlapping pillows, checkered in cherry red and goldenrod yellow. I sit in a chair against the eastern wall. My eyes rest on the center candle, unlit on the table. The heart of the chapel, the heart of the community.

Here I stay for the next hour, holding Jo's story. I think of bombs and bereavement and building bridges of healing. I think of empathy and power and curiosity and trust. I think of all that it takes to meet your enemy and make him your friend. I think of how forgiveness is more complicated than we'd like it to be and how peace isn't a place but a process. I think of courage and conversations and Corrymeela. I think of the Croí, and the stories that shelter and shadow our hearts. I think of Jo and Pat and all the stories I've heard so far.

And I wonder which ones I'll hear next, as I leave this island next week for an entirely new experience: South Africa.

8

WHEN RECONCILIATION MEANS NOTHING

Saul's left arm rests across his lap. He's my partner at the Ubuntu Symposium here in Cape Town, South Africa. This past week, I've lingered long enough at the offices of the Desmond and Leah Tutu Legacy Foundation that they've invited me to join for this daylong event. My group has been divided into pairs to discuss the challenges facing peace and democracy. For Saul, the challenges are personal.

"I was told I needed to make myself qualified," he tells me. "As a black man, I have a hard time, and I knew I had to make myself competitive. So I went to university. I got qualified. I got the résumé and skills. But it's been six years now, and I still can't get a job. I did what they said I needed to do and nothing has changed." He stops talking as tears fill his eyes. "And the worst part is," he says, "this government that said it was *for us* does nothing to help."

Within a minute, the group leader gathers the pairs back into the whole and asks us to share what we discussed. The first person to speak up is a white woman across the table. She's probably in her midfifties. She offers her story of pain and courage in hopes it can "provide inspiration" to the rest of us. She has no idea what Saul just told me. She tells us her story of leaving her abusive husband after far too many years as "his housewife." She says, "I had no qualifications. I was forty. Everyone said I could never get a job. But I tried anyway. I had to, for my kids. So with no qualifications, I applied to a job in finance. And I got it! I then moved up the ladder and was very successful." She's sitting on the edge of her seat, intensely, peering into our eyes as she scans our faces. She chronicles the "blessings" of her unexpected success. Then she says, "And if I can do it, you can too."

I sit stunned. I've just witnessed a remarkable example of how a sincere story can land in very unexpected ways. Sometimes our best intentions can have the worst impact. The woman assumes her story is universally applicable. In reality, it doesn't even apply to the people at this table.

THE CITY OF CAPE TOWN is as colorful and complex as its history. My bus from the international airport sped by a sea of pink flamingos, bathing in still waters, near the abject poverty of a township. I'm staying in a neighborhood known as the Kloof. Even though the legal separateness of the apartheid system ended in the 1990s, I'm finding it rare to see a person of color in this section of Cape Town, unless they are cooking or busing tables. Even if segregation isn't enforced by law, it can still be enacted by choice and consequence.

The beauty here is stunning. Table Mountain towers behind me; fishing and sailboats populate the waterfront below me.

Various shades of green and blue line the sea, sky, and surrounding hills, and the forty-minute walk down Long Street to the water leads me past myriad architectural styles, mostly Victorian and Cape Dutch. Many of these buildings are gorgeous, yet their beauty bothers me. They are a reminder of colonialism's legacy, of all the pain and suffering caused by the foreign invaders who sought to conquer and control this place. As this is my first trip to South Africa, I've spent my first few days blistering my feet, devouring museums, exploring neighborhoods, and enjoying the favorable exchange rate. It's good to be here.

I'M WAITING FOR MY NEXT INTERVIEW in the sunlit lobby of the Institute for Justice and Reconciliation (IJR).[1] Before I arrived in country, I emailed with the good people here about working from their offices and conducting some interviews. Over the last several days, their hospitality has held me with some much-needed warmth. I've been traveling for two months now, and the longing for home is gnawing. The friendly people here have helped.

Today I strolled my usual route down the tree-lined Government Avenue, past the Holocaust and Genocide Centre, to this simple white building with a gate in front. My conversation partner is a few minutes late. I pull out my phone to look through some of my photos from my time here so far.

On my third day, I wandered the waterfront and spotted the Robben Island Museum and launch site for ferries to the island. The next day, I took one out to the famous island prison where Nelson Mandela was incarcerated.

---

1. For more information about IJR, see www.ijr.org.za.

Entering the Robben Island compound immediately sent my mind back to Riverbend, the maximum security prison in Nashville where I volunteered for over four years before the warden banned me for organizing other volunteers to protest harmful policies of the Tennessee Department of Corrections. At Robben Island, I slowly walked the hallways lined with cells, flanked by scores of tourists, trying to pause long enough to breathe and reflect before the horde hurried me on. And then I saw Nelson Mandela's cell. I hung back from the group as people exited the cell block, and I peered through the bars. My stomach churned as I considered that Mandela spent eighteen years of his life in that very cell. Eighteen years.

JUST OVER A DECADE after apartheid was set in stone as national law in South Africa, Mandela grew disillusioned with the possibility that nonviolent resistance could free his homeland. Pass laws, through which the apartheid government forced black residents to carry identification passbooks at all times, had just been expanded. Control and harassment measures like this, standard procedure for most colonial enterprises, fanned the flames of resistance. In March 1960, thousands gathered at the local police station in Sharpeville without their passbooks, offering themselves up for arrest. The accounts of what happened next are contested, but the end result is clear: police killed sixty-nine people, including more than twenty children. Many were shot in the back as they fled.

The Sharpeville Massacre, as it's known, pushed Mandela into a new phase of resistance, and he cofounded uMkhonto we Sizwe (Spear of the Nation, or MK), the armed wing of the black liberation movement known as the African National

Congress. The sabotage and guerilla tactics of MK led to Mandela's arrest, sentencing, and twenty-seven-year incarceration.

STILL IN HIS CELL, I could see all the furnishings given Mandela upon arrival: a bowl, a cup, a toilet bucket, and a thin mat and blanket for sleeping on the floor. In his cell, he exercised and read, keeping his body and mind active, believing the tide would turn and that his and his friends' freedom would come with the freedom of all oppressed South Africans. As I scanned the stone cage, I thought of how those who served as guards at the prison now find themselves on the wrong side of history. I wondered if all those serving institutions of mass incarceration will one day be scrutinized for participating in the inhumane warehousing of human lives.

Flipping through my phone as I wait for the interview, I see a photo of a stone wall in the courtyard outside Mandela's cell block. Our guide had stopped there for a moment. He himself had served time on Robben Island, overlapping with Mandela for five years. He pointed to a corner wall.

"They would beat us here," he said. "Once they made a lash, they focused all their strikes on that first lash. They made us bleed, and then they poured iodine on it. We would cry. We would call for our mothers to rescue us, but our mothers never came." He paused. "We do not forgive for the sake of the men that did this to us. We forgive for the sake of our children. We must create a new future for them."

MY INTERVIEW TODAY at IJR is with Eleanor du Plooy, the project leader for the Ashley Kriel Youth Leadership Development Project. When Eleanor walks in, she smiles warmly and leads me into an unadorned meeting room, where we quickly lose ourselves in conversation. Half an hour slips by before I bother to switch on the recorder. When I finally do, she has just mapped out the tremendous work of the Ashley Kriel Project, which is named in honor of an anti-apartheid youth activist who was killed by South African police in 1987. The project is filled with programs she says are "fostering critical thinking among young people and giving them space to engage with issues of the past, helping them to position themselves in the present, and giving them the tools to think about the future."[2]

One of the ways they think about the future is through the lens of reconciliation, a term many people associate with South Africa. Eleanor tells me that the word carries weight for her, but that this year she has been "problematizing" it.

"How have you been doing that?" I ask.

"So first," she says, "what we did was ask, 'When you hear the word *reconciliation*, what do you think about it? What does it mean to you?' It was interesting again to hear what so many young people have been saying: that it is out of touch with the reality of what's actually needed currently. A lot of young people kind of associated reconciliation with not only whitewashing the past but sweeping things under the rug. People associated reconciliation with a denial of the black experience and black pain. I must be honest with you, I wasn't surprised by any of it, but it wasn't nice to hear either."

Here it is again—this idea of the "inappropriate conversation." The conversation of reconciliation—for the professor in Palestine, for Ali Abu Awwad to a degree, and now for the experiences of black youth in Cape Town—is experienced as a conversation primarily interested in overlooking pain,

---

2. As of this writing, Eleanor is now senior project leader at IJR.

ignoring problems, and denying patterns of injustice. For them, the hope of reconciliation has fizzled out as naive promises of ungrounded dreamers.

"Yeah," Eleanor adds, "a lot of people are very anti-reconciliation and anti-key figures who promoted reconciliation—people like the former president Nelson Mandela, who a lot of people see as a sellout. A lot of young people associate what he did with kind of selling out the majority of black people for political compromise."

While I did not expect to hear that, I am not too surprised either. I have a question to ask her now, though I think I know the answer. "How does that perspective compare with the way young white people see Mandela?" I ask.

She lifts her eyebrows. "Complete opposite," she says with a nod. "He becomes this almost demigod-like figure." It sounds like many white South Africans whitewash Mandela in the way many white Americans do Dr. Martin Luther King.

"Why do you think that is?" I ask, a bit facetiously.

"You know why!" she laughs, calling my bluff.

She's probably right, and I pause for a moment to consider how I want to respond. Before I do, Eleanor keeps going. She tells me how despite President Mandela's long legacy of social justice and social transformation, he toned that rhetoric down during the transition out of apartheid.

"Look," she says, "at that time, I can completely understand. I recognize why it was important to go a particular route, but I do believe a lot more work needed to be done. Social justice and social transformation should never have taken a back seat, because it completely delegitimized the reconciliation agenda, where it is today. I think it was convenient for them at that time to embrace *particular* aspects of who he was and what he stood for. I think it is only now that people are actually talking about Nelson Mandela as the freedom fighter, as being radical not just in his thinking, but in his *doing*."

She takes a breath, considering how to say her next point.

"So yeah, the reason why white South Africans have embraced reconciliation is because of the way it was positioned. And the way in which they made sense of it was, 'Let's keep everything the way it is, and let's talk about how we can go forward without real conversations about real change.' And I'm talking about *real* change in terms of things like *land distribution*. I'm talking about black economic empowerment."

All this resonates with the past, politics, and pain of home. It echoes the disillusionment I've heard from people of color about how dialogue surrounding "racial reconciliation" too often props up the status quo. *Real change*, as Eleanor said, is what's needed. Dialogue, relationship building, humanizing encounters—I do believe these are essential. And still, we cannot assume, for instance, that had Aryan Germans only come to *know* Jewish people, the Holocaust would never have happened. Reconciling relationships cannot be ignored; and it's also not enough. We cannot be interested only in forgiveness, kindness, empathy, and compassion; we must also consider things like power, generational trauma, redistribution of resources, reparations for harm, economic empowerment, and what to do with four hundred years of grieving. Advocates of reconciliation and advocates of justice must work together as colleagues, or we may, quite ironically, fight one another like enemies.

"What obstacles to reconciliation do you see economic disparities presenting?" I ask Eleanor.

"I will go out on a limb and say that is *the* problem," she answers. "This is not saying that race isn't the issue; it's just that race and economics are like *this*," and she interlocks her fingers. "It doesn't matter how far we've gone in the conversation about reconciliation, we come to this deadlock, to this wall that we keep hitting, where people say, 'But why is it that I have to live in a shack with a paraffin lamp, while my peer drives the latest BMW and lives in that house?' It comes to that—*every, single, time.*

"And I think at this point," she continues, "that's the biggest roadblock this social inequality and injustice is presenting: it continues to dehumanize people. If you feel dehumanized all the time and you can see it being played out in ways in which your family members see themselves and their position in the world—in relation to white people, in relation to people of power—and you are fortunate to have the opportunity to interrogate these things and be able to see it for what it is: there's no way that you're not going to be angry. So this whole thing of 'black rage' that people have now come to call it, it's almost kind of a natural response."

"Yes," I say. "We talk about 'black rage' in the States as well. On the one hand, the way people often use that phrase is full of judgment, dismissal, and condemnation. We often think of people who are raging as being out of control and irrational, and so by labeling it as 'black rage,' white people are able to act like, 'Oh, they're just overreacting.' Whereas on the other hand, it's like, *of course* there's rage. Look at the history of this. Everyone should be raging. Yet it does seem like that term was crafted by white people because so many of us want to be able to say, 'Well, here they go again.'"

"Exactly," she says. "You're angry, and you feel that as a human being this isn't right." Eleanor shares the example of an informal settlement nearby, where she read that around two thousand people are forced to share a single outdoor toilet.

"I mean, really," she says, "it's dehumanizing."

TWO DAYS AGO, I saw this very thing. I signed up for a guided walk-through of the Langa township, led by a local man named Sibu. He told me Langa was built for male migrant workers in 1901 just outside Cape Town. When apartheid legislation known as the Group Areas Act became law in 1950, many mixed racial communities in Cape Town were divided, their homes bulldozed, and many black families displaced into segregated townships. To enter "white" areas—the boundaries of which were constructed and determined by the apartheid government and represented the majority of the country, including its metropolitan areas—you had to receive permission from the authorities and carry an identification passbook. Failure to obey such rules could result in beatings, exile, and even imprisonment.

The apartheid government patrolled these townships like watchdogs, Sibu told me. Black people could use the streets and sidewalks only at certain times and could travel only in ones or twos. The white authorities stationed themselves throughout these communities to find "lawbreakers" and "bring them to justice." They controlled every aspect of life for the people confined to the townships. Living conditions. Access to mobility and employment. Freedoms of speech and assembly. Even how one could *identify* was controlled through predetermined categories.

Sibu guided me along a street passing through rows of yellow brick hostels with courtyards full of colorful laundry flapping on clotheslines. After fifteen minutes, we entered one of the informal settlements Eleanor just referenced. The language of *settlement* means something different to me given my experiences in the West Bank. The only vocabulary I had to conceptualize what I saw was *slum*, as controversial as that term is. Some 150,000 people living in one and a half square miles.

Residents there live with no electricity or running water. Thousands of people share a handful of dilapidated public toilets. Hand-emptying buckets is the form of flushing. Some of the homes even sit in marshes, as they have nowhere else to build.

Everything Sibu showed me served as an indictment of white supremacy. Because that's what this is truly about. It's about an ideology constructed by and for people who consider themselves "white." This isn't to say there is any inherent fault in people born with light skin, just as there's no inherent fault in dark skin. The curse isn't the skin color but rather the ideology that claims that "white" skin makes someone better, more deserving of power, more pure and holy and dignified and dominant. For those of us who are white, it's an ideology that believes our whiteness makes us supreme.

This way of thinking has always and will always suppress black and brown bodies. White supremacy is committed to keeping its own on the throne.

"I KNOW YOU SAID the young people you work with aren't all that interested in talking about reconciliation," I say to Eleanor. "So what do they prefer to talk about?"

"They're talking a lot about decolonization," she says. "Because decolonization says that fundamentally, structurally, the foundation of things is wrong. Things aren't working, so we need to completely change them, which is a very radical way of looking at it."

"*Decolonization* is a word that actually diagnoses the problem even as it's naming the solution," I add.

"Exactly," Eleanor says. "And we've never really spoken about it—this whole thing of colonization and slavery and apartheid and the oppression of people of color by white people. Yes, we had the Truth and Reconciliation Commission, which was important, and I don't think anybody should delegitimize the role the TRC played in the collective consciousness of South Africa at that time and even now. But there's never been a *real* dialogue," she stresses. "And if we think about dialogue, it has to be a sustained process over time. It can't just be a one-off thing. And if there's no conversation, there can be no recognition and no acknowledgment. And sometimes that's not *all* that people need, but as a basic entry point, that is what they need. They need acknowledgment."

If the legendary South African TRC has not had the impact of creating "real dialogue" in South Africa, then I'd wager we're not even close in the United States. We've never had a truth and reconciliation commission to deal with slavery or Jim Crow or the genocide of Indigenous peoples. We never had trials and accountability for enslavers. We never had effective, expansive, and equitable polices of reparation and resource redistribution away from families and institutions whose wealth was won on the backs of enslaved people. White society wanted to move on. Of course it did. Why on earth would it want to reckon with its violence?

Eleanor tells me that a major obstacle to having real dialogue is convincing white people to take part. She sees a real fear spring up in white South Africans, wondering what the consequences will be for "dredging up" issues of the past.

"Right," I say. "They may wonder, 'What do I have to admit? What do I have to give up? What changes for me?'"

"And what does this say about me?" she says. "People don't want to come, and that's such a huge problem in this work. But for me, proximity plays a huge role in how people perceive the other and themselves. That's going to be one of the first things we need to address if we want to break down these barriers and really talk about reconciliation. We need to come together. We need to *sit across* from each other. Dialogue and proximity play a huge role."

Eleanor and I begin to wonder aloud what might persuade reluctant white folks to enter these necessary conversations. She shakes her head and tells me that even needing to ask this question makes her angry.

"Because why do we have to incentivize people to get them into the room?" she says. "This is something that *needs* to happen, just on a very human level. We are human beings. If we have to think about what reconciliation really means, it's impossible to say we are reconciled if social inequality persists. It's impossible—because then reconciliation means nothing."

I wholeheartedly agree. This has been my sense this whole trip, seeing the tensions emerging between ideas of reconciliation and justice. They cannot exist without the other. When we think of social justice as dealing with inequality and inequity, reconciliation will sink without a foundation of social justice to stand on.

"It's like this thing of freedom," she continues, "and it can become very abstract, but you can't be free if somebody else isn't, because then you are not free as a human being. Say, for instance, on a very basic level, like what you mentioned with white Americans waking up to injustices in your country because you are afraid—that means that you've never really been free."

I feel an urge to snap my fingers in affirmation. "You *think* that you were free, but you weren't," she says. "You know, here in South Africa, they call it *swart gevaar*. And *swart gevaar*, if you translate it into English, basically means 'black danger.' The 'black danger' is always the specter haunting you, and so you're never going to be free, because it's always there so long as they aren't free and aren't enjoying the same life you are."

This language opens wide in me an understanding of my own embedded racial biases. It helps me understand why I immediately get nervous if I'm on a quiet street at night and a black man approaches, whereas the sight of a white man doesn't alarm me in the same way. I reason with myself quickly, but my body has already tensed. It's because the culture of white supremacy in which I've been swimming all my life has taught me an easy narrative: white people are safe; black people are not. This narrative of the dangerousness of blackness has everything to do with the abominable treatment of people of color before and since the origin of the United States.

For example, just to remind us:

1. During the trans-Atlantic slave trade (ca. 1525–1866), European colonizers kidnapped and forcibly shipped over twelve million Africans to "the New World." One-quarter of those were children.

2. In 1860, at the beginning of the Civil War, more than four million black people were in the United States. Less than 489,000 were free; 90 percent were enslaved.

3. After the abolition of plantation slavery, white Americans still forced black people into labor through a system known as convict leasing. If convicted of a crime, black people again could be forced to work without pay. This system was made possible by the Thirteenth Amendment to the U.S. Constitution, which allows for slavery if the person is convicted of a crime.

4. Between the end of the Civil War and 1950, more than four thousand black people were murdered by white people in racial terror lynchings, mostly in the South.[3]

3. Thanks to professor Henry Louis Gates Jr. for this research, reported in Henry Louis Gates Jr., "Slavery, by the Numbers," *The Root*, February 10, 2014, https://www.the root.com/slavery-by-the-numbers-1790874492; as well as the Equal Justice Initiative's

5. Black adults make up 12 percent of the U.S. population but 33 percent of the prison population.[4]

ONCE, IN NASHVILLE, I learned of a kind of truth-and-justice hearing at a local university. A friend of mine had helped organize it. It was an opportunity for some public truth-telling on issues of race and policing. So I went to listen.

One of the first speakers was a black man I'll call Jay. He was a former police and correctional officer. Jay stood while he addressed those gathered. "We have a problem with the culture of policing," he said. "It's a scary job. I often had to walk up on houses and such, and you never know what's going to happen. You're conditioned to assume the worst. It's a very real fear and a very real threat. The training we get trains you to be fearful of the people you're supposed to protect and serve." In fact, I heard that day that police, on average, spend seven times as many hours training to *shoot* as training to *deescalate*. I heard that in the previous year, police killed at least two unarmed black people *every week*, and that black people are three times more likely to be killed by police than white people are.[5] "In fear," Jay said, "you don't value the person as a person; you see them as an opponent, a threat. And at the end of the day, I know it's highly unlikely I'll be convicted or even indicted. We have a saying that we'd rather be tried by twelve than carried by six. So if I feel like there's a situation

---

Lynching in America: Confronting the Legacy of Racial Terror, 3rd. ed. (Montgomery, AL: Equal Justice Initiative, 2017), https://lynchinginamerica.eji.org/report/.

4. John Gramlich, "The Gap between the Number of Blacks and Whites in Prison Is Shrinking," Pew Research Center, updated April 30, 2019, https://www.pewresearch .org/fact-tank/2019/04/30/shrinking-gap-between-number-of-blacks-and-whites-in- prison/. These figures are from 2017.

5. These statistics are corroborated at "Police Killed More Than 100 Unarmed Black People in 2015," Mapping Police Violence, accessed October 16, 2019, https://mapping policeviolence.org/unarmed/.

where someone's going to die, you better believe I plan to be going home that night."

Another man spoke. He was a black man and a preacher and said he was in his home preparing for his sermon the next morning. He realized he'd left a book in his car, so he hurried outside to get it. He was barefoot, wearing jeans and a T-shirt, belt undone, with his gate open, door open, and porch light on. The lights of a police car flashed, and officers stepped out and demanded he get on the ground so they could search him. They thought he was breaking into the car—which was his—in front of the nice house—which he owned.

"It's too much to wake up in the morning," the preacher said, "wondering if you're going to make it back home some-time, and wondering if your kids are going to make it back home safe. I often fear I'll be mistaken for somebody who looks even a little like me."

He paused and shook his head. Then he nearly whispered, as if letting us in on a secret, "We're behind on getting to know each other."

At this same school not long before, I had heard antiracism educator and writer Robin DiAngelo speak. Among the many brutal and necessary diagnoses she offered on racism in the United States, she cited the continued segregation of American lives, especially as it relates to education. I recall her saying something along these lines: Almost all of us in the United States have been taught by white people, who were taught by white people, who were taught by white people, and so on. And these white people learned from textbooks mostly written *by* white people *for* white people. Our all-consuming white-washed lives convey to us that people of color have nothing of value to offer.

As I walked back to my car that night, I began thinking back to my own education, from kindergarten through graduate school. I calculated that in all my years of education in academic institutions, I have learned from approximately sixty teachers. Then I had an alarming realization: Not one of those teachers was black. All, save one, were white.

"YOU KNOW," I SAY TO ELEANOR, "with this whole conversation on reconciliation—I understand why people with privilege and power are afraid to engage in it. I think that *true* reconciliation threatens the power structures. Reconciliation needs to be dealing with creating healthy, right relationships, which must mean dealing with power imbalances. Inequality in power, access, distribution of resources—all these tear at any hope of deep relationship. If there are to be right relationships created, there must be a leveling of power. Therefore the people on top *should*, in a way, be nervous about this conversation, because it's going to mean giving something up. So that, to me, is the big challenge in bringing people of power and privilege into the conversation."

"And you know," Eleanor says, "sometimes white people who want to do good work ask me, 'So what can I do?' And the thing is—go and have conversations within your groups. Have in-group conversations with other white people and change it from the inside. You are most familiar with how this structure works, how the conversations go, and the language to use. So go use it."

I'M PUSHING UP against the edge of the time Eleanor said she had for our conversation. I still have scores of questions I'd like to discuss with her, but I land on a final one: What's next for the healing of South Africa?

"Well," she says, "I think the vision for what South Africa could be should still be the vision. There was nothing wrong with the vision. South Africa belongs to all people. Whether it's black or whether it's white, it belongs to everybody. We just now need to think of ways in which we can facilitate that. First, I think one of the ways would be social justice in general, in terms of just restoring people's dignity. Second would be to rehumanize the other. We need to see each other as human beings. And I do think dialogue would be important. We need to talk." She smiles, glances away, and then turns her eyes back to mine. "We need to reintroduce ourselves to each other."

9

LIKE A POISON

Themba Lonzi sits softly in front of me. His faded beige jacket makes his red polo pop with color. His wisdom is large, yet he speaks with such gentleness that I need to sit forward if I'm to hear anything. I am struck by his collectedness and calm, especially for a man who grew up black in apartheid South Africa, enduring and witnessing all kinds of violence. I know Themba was active in African National Congress resistance to the white apartheid government during his younger years, and I know that now he's active in reconciliation work. I want to know what happened.

I'm back at the IJR offices—in the library this time—as I listen to Themba. He tells me he grew up in the 1970s with a large family in a small home in the Gugulethu township outside Cape Town. In that home, he remembers no talk of apartheid. No real conversations on what was happening in the country or why. But the silence in the home about apartheid clashed with the clamor of its reality outside. Police sirens. Gunshots. Fires. Armored vehicles. Growing up, Themba couldn't escape the impact of apartheid on the streets, though he didn't even know its name. Without conversations at home to give context for what was happening on the streets, he couldn't make sense of it all.

In primary school in the 1980s, he began hearing from other students about "the movement" and a system called apartheid that was designed to control every aspect of their lives. All on the basis of their skin color. Where he lived, where he could go, whom he could and couldn't marry, whether he could vote—all this was determined for him as a black person by the white minority of his country. A fire kindled in his bones, he joined in protest marches as a young student and witnessed firsthand the police brutality that marked apartheid and continues to plague too many countries today, including my own. He and his friends met the violence of police with resistance. They threw stones and destroyed government property. Anything that represented the government oppressing them was a target. Attack it all, they believed. And the response from the apartheid police was to shoot. Sometimes they shot teargas. Other times they shot live bullets.

And so there were funerals. Many, many funerals.

"One of the images that has stayed with me for a long time," Themba says, "is the image of carrying coffins. We carried them through the streets of Gugulethu to the gravesite to bury them. And these were coffins of teenagers. Some of these young people were not even clear what was happening around them but became part of the anger that the youth like me were experiencing at the time."

I am hearing echoes of Palestine as he talks.

Themba came of age with fear and rage toward the police and their systemic abuses of power. The times that police officers beat him personally were like pouring gas on the flames. The anger turned toward hatred, and the hatred spread beyond the police. Themba found himself hating white people in general, anyone and anything that symbolized—in truth or theory—the perpetuation of pain on his people. Anytime he rode the train from Gugulethu to Cape Town, apartheid was on display. The squashed, sardine-like housing of his neighborhood gradually opened into spacious, beautiful homes and areas nearer the city. This is where the white folks lived, and he could never understand why the people who looked like him were forced to live in such poverty while others rested in such comfort. This humiliation propelled his hatred as he came to believe that police weren't the only enemy; all white people were guilty.

When he tells me this, I remember another story I've heard of Gugulethu.

IN 1993, as South Africa prepared for its transition out of apartheid into the Mandela-led African National Congress government, tensions rose, violence increased, and white-led security forces continued killing people. American Fulbright scholar Amy Biehl lived in South Africa during this time. An outspoken, passionate activist for equal rights and racial justice, Amy refused to attend an all-white university during her time in Cape Town.

One day, she visited Gugulethu with some friends. Amid their deep and justifiable anger toward apartheid, several young black men attacked and stabbed Amy to death. Her whiteness represented to them—as it did for Themba—the system that was oppressing and killing them. During the years the Truth and Reconciliation Commission (TRC) was in session, these men, then incarcerated for her murder, applied for amnesty. Under the TRC rules, if you applied for amnesty, told the full truth, and your violence was politically motivated, you could be considered for pardon. In these hearings, Amy's parents found a voice, and the footage of those interactions is powerful.

As the men listened to Amy's parents speak of their daughter, they soon acknowledged that they did not know the woman they killed. They saw her as just another white oppressor. They confessed that had they known what kind of person she was, they would not have killed her.

These men eventually received amnesty, and Amy's parents established the Amy Biehl Foundation, hoping to carry on the good work to which she had dedicated her life. A few of the men who killed Amy were hired to work for the foundation.

IN 1995, after South Africa had officially moved into democracy, Themba was a student in an arts institution studying theater as a tool for community development—work he continues today. He had just formed a theater group when he was approached by interfaith leaders from the Religious Response to the Truth and Reconciliation Commission. Upon learning that the scale of the TRC would not be able to let everyone's stories be heard, these religious leaders began charting a workshop process that could run parallel to the TRC hearings. They hoped these workshops, which eventually became the work of the organization Healing of Memories, would foster safe spaces for people on all sides of apartheid to tell their stories to each other. This, the leaders thought, might decrease the alienation that leads to prejudice and violence and might ultimately bring healing. They wanted Themba to develop a theater component that could be used at the start of every workshop.[1]

"So for us," Themba says, speaking of the students who were performing the community theater, all of whom were black, "this is a good opportunity to be commissioned to put together some work. And this meant the generation of some income for us as well."

Themba and the other students set out to gather personal stories from people who had experienced the apartheid years. They stretched themselves to listen to and eventually perform the stories of white people's experiences during apartheid—not because they wanted to, but because this was the job they were hired to do.

"I remember the first one we performed," he tells me. "Normally, soon after the performance, the actors would be given an opportunity to say how it feels to present a story like that. It is like an emotional roller coaster presenting the stories. And the participants would have an opportunity to share how they felt while they were listening and watching us perform. They described feelings of anger, feelings of pain, feelings of guilt and shame, resentment—all those mixed feelings." After Themba's theater group performed on the opening night of the workshop, they would go home and leave the participants and the facilitators to continue together.

"But I became more interested," Themba says, "and I spoke with my colleagues and the workshop leaders and said I wanted to stay for the full two-and-a-half-day residential workshop. And I deliberately said I wanted to stay because I knew that I had my own stuff that I had to deal with from

<hr />

1. For more on the Institute for the Healing of Memories, see www.healing-memories.org.

growing up in apartheid." So at the next opportunity, Themba made arrangements to be part of the full workshop.

"I performed on the first night," he says, "and the second night is where we break into smaller groups. This is where most of the storytelling takes place. And I remember when it was my time to share my personal experience, I was asking myself a lot of questions: How are the people going to respond when I tell them what my experiences are? Will I be judged? And then all the 'what ifs.' So at that first workshop, I really only told *part* of my story. Not all. Because I was really gauging whether this is a safe environment for me to tell, to bare it all, to tell everything."

So Themba told part of his story about living under apartheid. But he held back. He was careful about how much he shared and how much of his pain he let people see. He realized after the conversation, however, that people had actually listened—carefully, with compassion. Themba decided he could reveal more. "So I asked if I could attend the same workshop a second time," he says. "And even at the first one, I felt I had begun to offload stuff that had really become distracting in my life, stuff that would really make me lose focus. Because I was still battling a lot of anger because of what I experienced, because of friends I lost."

Themba then tells me of one of his friends who was brutally murdered by a group called the Red Dukes. His friend was so mangled that Themba and the others with him could identify him only by his shoes. His story reminds me of some of the nightmares I've heard of the Shankill Butchers mutilating Catholics in West Belfast during the Troubles. Or of the lynching of Emmitt Till and thousands of others.

"How did your friends, the people you grew up with, respond to your initial involvement in these kinds of reconciliation processes?" I ask him.

He looks to the side for a moment to remember. "Some guys I was with when we were still in youth and fighting in the streets in protest would say, 'Oh Themba, you are trying to make us soft now.' For me, yes, I was angry during the years of apartheid. Even in the early 1990s, I was still angry and bitter. I had some desire for revenge. I mean, I've lost people—you know, friends. People I grew up with have died. I've seen the humiliation our parents experienced. I've learned about what our grandparents have been through."

And still, it seems for Themba, the skepticism of his friends wasn't enough to deter him from the journey on which he now found himself. He was wanting change—not just socially or politically in South Africa, but internally, for himself.

"I realized I was carrying a lot of anger and bitterness and hatred inside of me because of the things I've seen, because of what I've experienced. But"—he pauses for a moment, nodding ever so slightly—"I realized that the anger and the pain—the bitterness—was not hurting anybody else. It was destroying *me*; it was inside *me*. Inside, living like a poison that's eating me up alive. I chose to say, 'I'm going to take a route of releasing this poison out of my system.' And of course, it is a long journey. It is not a short process."

SOMETIMES THE SIMPLEST IDEAS are the most novel. Like, what if every emotion exists because we need it? And what if each emotion is telling us something important about ourselves and what we need to do? Educator and researcher Karla McLaren's incredibly helpful book *The Art of Empathy* has opened a whole new way for me to understand emotions. Rather than pathologize emotions like anger and shame, McLaren explains that *every* emotion is necessary. And because we need them, every emotion requires some kind of action. Anger, for instance, serves as a kind of border guard. It activates when some boundary of the self has been crossed. It tells us to take action to protect our sense of self or that of others.

McLaren also notes that while every emotion is important, if we allow any one emotion to dominate us, it can turn toxic. This is particularly true when a dominant emotion overwhelms us to the point that we desire to harm others. Sometimes holding on to an emotion for too long hurts more than it helps.

This way of thinking about emotions seems to fit some of Themba's story. The anger he lived with for much of his life wasn't just important; it was absolutely necessary. Anger was exactly the right response to the kind of barbaric violations suffered under the apartheid regime of South Africa. He needed that anger to take action to resist the injustices being beaten down on his community. And just as McLaren warned, as Themba's anger lived with him, it began to feel cancerous—"like a poison," he called it—so that it was no longer serving him the way it once did. Once the anger metastasized into hatred, it became another weapon of the apartheid system.

"SO THE PROCESS of really being able to tell my story," Themba continues, "and to be able to listen to other people's stories from different communities began to allow me an opportunity to deal with some of the most painful, most difficult emotions I was carrying. And of course in that process, you don't listen to things that you agree with. You will be in a small group with someone who was in the army, and you will feel you are boiling because you know that these were probably some of the people sent to the township to shoot us. So you're sitting in this group listening to the story. And you listen to maybe another person who comes from the Coloured community sharing their experiences as well—of forced removal, of the brutality of the police, of constant protest, and the killing of activists and the disappearances.[2]

"But I think what I found was really beneficial was that I started to feel lighter. Because I began to share things that I never shared with anybody. I think when you start to be brutally honest and share some of your deepest prejudices and some of your deepest stereotypes, you begin to feel lighter, and you begin to *challenge* your own prejudices. Because at the time when we were growing up, we didn't hear stories about people in the white communities who were activists within their communities. You wouldn't see them coming in, being part of the protests. But they were playing a role in their own communities. So you grow up with an understanding that every person who is white is oppressing us in this country. But when you begin to learn about the role other people played from those communities that you see as your enemy, you begin to question the whole generalization, the whole notion of pre-judging people."

I think it's important to say here that questioning the validity of generalizing a group of people is not equivalent to saying white South Africans weren't complicit in apartheid. Of course they were. They weren't all guilty in equal ways, but everyone who benefits from an unjust system and is not actively working to dismantle it is at least partly responsible for its harm. The same is true in Israel. The same is true in the United States.

---

2. *Coloured* is a commonly used term in South Africa that refers to people of certain mixed racial heritage. It does not carry the same connotation there as it does in the United States.

It's true everywhere. Generalizations do little to help us. And neither do naive assertions of clean hands.

THEMBA'S JOURNEY into the work of reconciliation—work he stumbled into "by accident," he said—was propelled by a desire to heal from emotions that exhausted and emptied him. And unsurprisingly, the healing he's found has come through opening himself up to the stories of others. His story, like those of so many others I've met, hinges on empathy. On curiosity. On *staying in the room.* The work of reconciliation is the work of struggling to say the difficult things to one another in such a way that you can stay in the room together. And if you must leave, reconciliation is the commitment to come back and try again. That's what I hear in his story.

And I also hear in his story the same thing I heard in the email from the Palestinian professor at the beginning of my trip, in the words of Ali Abu Awwad and Dr. Zoughbi at Wi'am, and in my earlier conversation with Eleanor. And that's this: Any process of reconciliation that hopes to keep people in the room but doesn't address the obstacles preventing them from getting to the room in the first place is not a process worth anyone's time. Emotions, distrust, grievances—these aren't the only roadblocks to reconciliation. And Themba sees firsthand all the complicated practical problems to uncomplicated processes of reconciliation.

"When we offer a workshop," he says, "we would have a follow-up session, maybe three weeks later, with the same people. Each person would get a chance to say how it's been since the workshop. For some people, they would say it was a life-changing experience. They would say it was a great opportunity for them to offload the burden they've been carrying for so long. It was a great opportunity to tell the stories that they'd never even told their parents, that they had kept for twenty years or more. And for some people, they would say, 'Yes, it was a great experience, but I went back to my reality of wondering how I'm going to put food on the table for my kids. How am I going to get work? How am I going to send my kids to university? How do I clothe my children? How do I protect them in that environment we live in? Because we live in pretty violent communities.'

"And so you find out that people take three steps forward when they're part of a reconciliation process, and then they go back to reality and take two steps back. What does that say to us? It says there's an urgency that is needed in terms of addressing the economic imbalances. We can talk nice reconciliation talk at a workshop, but I go back and try and look through the crumbs and see what I'm going to eat. And you go back and enjoy your croissants with strawberry jam in your nice home. So the fundamental human needs of the people should go hand in hand. It shouldn't be either/or. The reconciliation process is good at dealing with issues of the heart and being able to connect with people that you would not have thought you could connect with. This process is very important, because people can get all the material things they need and that wouldn't help us to create the society we really want. But if we balance all the fundamental human needs—access to education, job creation, access to healthcare—and we balance this with processes that are helping to bring people together, we will definitely see a much greater impact in terms of social cooperation in South Africa."

Reconciliation that isn't interested in the injustices that are dividing people is shallow at best and sinister at worst. And any effort at justice that addresses the basic needs of security and sustenance but pays little attention to the quality of compassionate relationship between people is like trying to build the frame of a ship without any adhesive. I'm with Themba—these pursuits must always go hand in hand.

"People *really* want to be part and parcel of this process, but there are very few spaces where South Africans can have an honest conversation about the issues dividing us," Themba says. "There are very few spaces. So the whole issue of economic imbalances in South Africa is beginning to create problems for us, because you cannot continue going to people and saying, 'Let's find ways of reconciling with one another in South Africa' while people are confronted by issues of daily survival. For some people, they want to be part of these processes, but they say, 'Man, I have to go and find some work. I must find fees to pay for my kids to go to school. I must get transport,' and so on. The list is long."

So Themba tells me he believes it's important to challenge the "touch and go" programs too common in reconciliation efforts. "I believe there is a need for more long-term processes," he says. "And I think what needs to be included are programs about community upliftment. I mean, in South Africa, the reality is that we have people in poor communities. And we have people with a lot of money; people who are rich and well-off. And what I always say is we will never really be free if the majority of the people are poor in this country. Those who are rich and perceived rich will never feel safe, because those who are poor will make sure, by any means necessary, to get what they want."

I'm now hearing an echo of Eleanor's sentiment about the white fear of the "specter of black danger," the notion that white people aren't free as long as black people are consistently poor because we white folks will always be glancing over our shoulder to see if the people we and our ancestors stole from have finally come to settle up.

Themba talks about the amount of money that white people in Cape Town spend on home security measures, such as security gates, electric wires, and armored sports cars. "People spend a lot of their money on security, and you can't say we are free when you are in your own house but you live like you are in a prison," he says. "Bars over the windows. Security cameras. That's not freedom. Those are the things that raise this question of how to reconcile an unequal society."

Themba and I circle these challenges for a while, giving example after example of the complications of doing this work we both believe in. After a while, I ask him, "Amid all these challenges, what would you say makes this work rewarding? Or even, *would* you say at this point that it *is* rewarding?"

"I am in reconciliation work," he says, with something like conviction. "It is a part of my life. It's more than just work, really; it's something I believe in. It's something I've experienced with people across communities, where you wish that other people could be in this room. I think the beauty about this work is that you begin in a way to reclaim your humanity. It's like you're becoming human again. Because I believe we are not born with hate and resentment and bitterness and desires for revenge, but it's experiences in the systems that have shaped us that fill people with all these negative feelings. But I believe when we begin to work with others—on reconciliation, nation-building, and healing—we begin in a way to become humans to one another."

"I'M WONDERING whether you have any words of wisdom you might like to offer regarding our struggles back in the

U.S.," I say. "Obviously, we had our own system of apartheid. And the same thing that you're seeing here I think we're seeing in the States—which is that the structures of apartheid were very well instituted and there is almost a degree of permanence to them. They are sticking around. With so many years of slavery, Jim Crow, and the like, those kinds of segregation and discrimination policies don't just disappear. People are still facing those in various forms. I wonder what you think is ahead for us in the States, what should we be thinking about, what should we be striving for."

Themba nods a few times, thinking. "I think one thing I've learned from looking at those experiences in the U.S. is what happens when injustices go unacknowledged. I've realized there's a difference between *knowledge* and *acknowledgment*. There are things that we know—in relationships and families and communities and nations—but no one dares to speak about them until there is some kind of explosion. There needs to be some form of acknowledgment of the challenges that people are confronted with in the different communities. There needs to be some courage in terms of the openness of dealing with these issues."

To know something is not the same as to acknowledge it. That's good language. We, as a nation, may *know* that slavery and lynching were awful and unjust and barbaric, but that does not mean we've *acknowledged* this in big, public, meaningful, responsible ways. The Equal Justice Initiative in Alabama is leading the way on this. They've built the first ever museum about lynching in the United States and are dedicated to erecting a monument at every known lynching site in America. This is the type of acknowledgment that might actually help us.

"The hope for me, the hope for South Africa, the hope for the U.S., and the hope for the world lies on ensuring that young people become part and parcel of shaping something different," Themba says. "Because I will tell you: it's much more difficult to try and change the older generation. Yes, there's a possibility of some of them changing how they view themselves and other people. But I think there's more hope in saying let's engage the young people, the students."

Themba begins to speak of "visiting history." My undergraduate degree is in history. I believe in the importance of knowing the past. And I'm fully on board when Themba says that visiting the past can be dangerous. We must always ask ourselves *why* we're going back to the stories of the past, because we can all put history to work for our own purposes. "Some people go back to make sure the anger and bitterness and desire for revenge are alive," he says. "It's like poking the wound so the blood keeps flowing. History has been used and will continue to be used as a reason to attack others and see them as targets. Extremists use history a lot to justify the horrible things they do to other people. So we need to be careful as to why we're going back there. We need to be clear that we are going back to *understand* the environment and what created that situation and the choices that individuals and communities made and what the consequences were of those choices. And I think when young people begin to understand that broader picture, they will be able to understand the importance of choice in shaping the different society.

"We can easily pass on our bitterness and anger and frustrations to the younger generations, and they find themselves having to deal with all these messages that are coming to them," Themba says. "We are selective in our memory of history, and selective memory is not helpful in issues of reconciliation and nation-building. If you select what you want to remember, you tend to remember the bad things that were done to you, the wrongs that came your direction, rather than looking at what things *we* could've done differently. What are things that were problematic that *we* were part of as well?"

ONE OF THE HARDEST TASKS of reconciling after conflict is making room, alongside your own version, for the *other's* version of the story of the conflict. We don't have to replace our narrative with someone else's, but rather must zoom out a bit. We have to expand the storyboard. Reconciliation doesn't need us to agree on all aspects of the story of our differences. If it did, nothing would ever improve. Instead, reconciliation allows us to acknowledge that there *are* other ways of telling the story and that those ways might hold some truth.

Themba's story models this well. And it reminds me of two other men I've met. This idea—of expanding the storyboard—takes me back to the beginning of my journey, to the heat of the conflict in Israel and Palestine. There I spoke with two men, one Israeli and one Palestinian, who have been catapulted to the edges of themselves. And it was precisely on this journey to the brink that they discovered this surprising truth: there is room for their enemy's story to find some shelter alongside their own.

10

CRACKS OF HOPE

Rami Elhanan looked different in person than I expected. I'm not sure why. I already knew a bit of Rami's story, and the bit I knew told me he was likely a sad man. Why wouldn't he be after his daughter was murdered?

We met in the open area in front of the Citadel in Jerusalem's Old City. He'd just parked his motorcycle inside Jaffa Gate, and I was coming up from David Street. The sunlight brightened his face. He had a clean look with a neat, short haircut. His button-up shirt was lined with white and gray vertical stripes, like one of mine. In fact, I'm quite sure I own the same shirt.

Rami led me up Latin Patriarch Street and into the Gloria Hotel. There was a relatively quiet dining lounge near the entrance. The Jerusalem stone walls had Moorish accents, and if the clocks hadn't read noon, the light of scattered lamps might have made me think it was twilight. Rami chose a spot against the wall, sitting on one of those classic red-and-black

patterned cushions you see everywhere in that part of the
world. We ordered an espresso for him and a mint lemonade
for me. After we each took a sip, he began his story, slowly.

"My name is Rami Elhanan. I am a sixty-five-year-old
retired graphic designer living in Jerusalem. I was born in Jerusalem, seventh generation, to my mother, who was born here
in the Old City. My father, who came to this country in 1946,
is a Holocaust survivor—right out of Auschwitz."

It didn't surprise me that Rami's father was at Auschwitz.
Many Israelis have family members who suffered the Nazis'
terror. As Robi Damelin told me, "If you don't understand that
part of Jewish history, you'll never understand the DNA of
fear." And it's that part of Rami's story—the part about fear
and what he did with it—that most inspires me.

"My story goes around one particular date of the Jewish
calendar, which is the day of Yom Kippur. You know, Yom Kippur for the Jews is the holiest day of the year. The day where
you ask forgiveness for your sins. On this very day, I was a very
young soldier fighting this horrible October '73 war. We started
it with a company of eleven tanks and finished with only three.
I've lost many good friends over there. I came out of the war
a very angry and bitter and disappointed young man, with a
determination to detach myself from any kind of commitment.
I got out of the army to finish my studies. Then I got married
and had four kids.

"On the very eve of Yom Kippur, September 1983, my
daughter was born here in Jerusalem, and her name was Smadar. The name Smadar is taken from the Bible, the Song of Sol-
omon. It means 'the grape of vine,' which means 'the opening
of the flower.' And she really was a sparkling and vivid and
joyful and beautiful and talented little girl. Everybody used to
call her 'the Princess.'" I remember seeing the hint of a smile

as Rami spoke of Smadar. Despite the pain, talking about his Princess obviously brought some sense of peace.

"She was really amazing," he went on, "an excellent student, a swimmer, a dancer. She played the piano. She was really amazing, and we lived a very good life. In a way, you could say that we put ourselves into a big bubble, completely detached from the outside world. This went on until about eighteen years ago."

I was fixed on every word.

"On September 4, 1997, a few [weeks] before Yom Kippur, this bubble of ours was blown up to millions of pieces by two Palestinian suicide bombers who blew themselves up on Ben Yehuda Street, which is about five minutes walking distance away from here." Rami paused for a few seconds, looking down at the floor. "They killed five people that day, including three little girls. One of them was my [nearly] fourteen-year-old Smadar. It was Thursday afternoon and the beginning of a very long and dark night which continues until today."

The noise around us grew louder as Rami wiped sweat from his mouth. People laughed and conversed in different corners of the room. I leaned in to hear better as he told me about the moments surrounding the murder of his daughter. How it started when he was on his way to the airport. The news came on the radio. Bombings in Jerusalem. Then the instinctive mental scan to remember where all your loved ones are. A moment of relief, of hope. Everyone should be okay. Then the call from home. Learning Smadar wasn't there. She was supposed to be babysitting her younger brother, Yigal. It was Nurit on the phone, Rami's wife. She said a friend of their son called. He had seen Smadar downtown with friends buying books for the new school year.

Downtown. Where Ben Yehuda Street is.

"Gradually," Rami said, "you find yourself running in the streets trying to find her. She completely vanished. You go from hospital to hospital and from police station to police station, many long and frustrating hours, until eventually—very, very late—you find yourself in the morgue . . . and you see this sight which you will never ever be able to forget for the rest of your life."

From the morgue, Rami went home. His home was filled with "thousands and thousands of people coming to pay respect and offer condolences." Then came the time for sitting shiva.

"These are the seven days of the Jewish mourning period," he said. "It was really an outstanding event, because the killing of this little girl made a big noise in Israel and around the world. She was the granddaughter of the late general, professor, and member of the Knesset Matti Peled."

"This is your father?" I asked.

"My wife's father," he said. "He was among the first people who understood that the very existence of the state of Israel will depend not on military power but its ability to lend a hand and create communication with the other side."

Smadar was buried beside her grandfather. The funeral was something to behold. Political giants attended. Prime ministers Ariel Sharon, Shimon Peres, and Yitzhak Rabin, all of whom had been friends of Matti Peled since the 1948 war, were there. Even representatives of Yasser Arafat and the newly established Palestinian Authority came. Rami said the news shook Israel like "an earthquake."

"There was one more fact that created a lot of noise," he told me. "My wife, Nurit, the daughter of this late general, was a schoolmate of Bibi Netanyahu, who was prime minister at the time." As of this writing, Benyamin Netanyahu is still the prime minister of Israel and has been as uninterested in making true peace as any Israeli leader to date. Liberal Israelis see him the way liberal Americans see Donald Trump.

"When he [Netanyahu] called her," Rami said, "she told Bibi, 'It's your fault. It's the fault of the occupation.'" I admire the courage of Nurit. To blame the death of your daughter on the foremost leader of your country is a bold act.

"I think it was the first time ever," Rami continued, "that victims of terror looked not only to the mosquito but to the swamp."

I don't think I'll ever forget that sentence—what it said, with such simplicity, about context, blame, responsibility, and cycles of violence. Nurit may rightly have blamed the suicide bombers who killed her daughter. Yet she also knew that had Israel's army not occupied Palestine, her daughter would almost certainly be alive.

As Rami and his family sat shiva, they grieved, receiving visitor after visitor as they tried to process what had just happened and what would happen next. And then, shiva ended. The seven days were up. It was time for the eighth day.

"The eighth day, everybody goes back to their normal, everyday business. And you are left alone. You need to wake up. You need to stand up and face yourself and make a decision about what to do now: this new unbearable burden on your shoulders, this new personality, and especially how to deal with the anger. Anger which eats you alive from within. You have to choose between two possible ways. The first one is obvious. When someone kills your fourteen-year-old little girl, you're so mad, you are so angry, that you want to get even—which is natural and understandable. And most people choose this way, the way of revenge and retaliation. This endless cycle of violence, which never stops. But we are people; we are not animals. We have heads on our shoulders, and we use them. You start to think; you start to ask yourself questions: 'Would killing anyone bring her back? Will causing pain to someone ease this pain?' And the answer is 'Certainly not.'

"So in a very gradual and complicated process, you come to the other option, which is trying to *understand* what happened here. Why did it happen? How could such a horrible thing take place? What can cause someone to be that angry, that mad, that *desperate*, that *hopeless*, that he is willing to blow himself up with a fourteen-year-old little girl?" He breathed. Then he said, "And next is the most important question of all: What can you do personally to prevent this unbearable pain from reaching other people?"

To ask yourself, in the chasms of your agony, what you can do to save others from the same pain: it's a stunning question. A courageous question. A risky question. A beautiful question. If my own child were killed, I hope that's the question I would ask myself in the days after the funeral.

"Well, it's not easy," he said. "It takes time."

Initially, Rami thought he might be able to go back to normal, to pretend all that just happened hadn't actually happened. But he couldn't, of course; he was different. Changed.

One year later, he met a stranger who changed his life. Rami told me the stranger's name was Yitzhak Frankenthal, the same man who approached Robi Damelin after her son David was killed by a Palestinian sniper.

"We started talking. He told me about his son Arik—a soldier who was kidnapped and murdered by Hamas in 1994—and about this organization that he created [the Parents Circle-Families Forum] for those who lost their loved ones and still work for peace."

At first Rami was furious at Yitzhak for his audacity to approach him in his grief. "I was so angry with him because I remembered he came to my house during the days of mourning a year before. I asked him, 'How could you do it? How could you step into someone's house who just lost a loved one and talk about peace? How dare you!' And he, being the great man that he is, was not insulted. He just invited me over to watch a meeting with this group of crazy people. I said okay. I got a little bit curious."

Rami went to the meeting but didn't fully engage at first. "I was standing aside," he said, "very detached, very reluctant, very cynical, as I always am. Watching those people who came down from the buses, people that for me, as an Israeli patriot, were always living legends. People I admired. And I never, ever thought that one day I would become one of them: the Israeli bereaved families. But what really made the difference was the sight of the Palestinian bereaved families. I was standing there watching them coming down from the buses looking toward me, shaking my hand for peace, hugging me, crying with me. I was so deeply moved and so deeply shocked.

"You see, I was forty-seven years old. I am ashamed to admit it was the first time ever in my life I had met Palestinians as human beings. Not as workers in the streets, not as 'terrorists.' Human beings—people who carry the same burden that I carry. People who suffer exactly like I suffer. I was so moved. I remember seeing this old Arab lady coming down from the bus with this long black traditional Palestinian dress. She had a picture of her six-year-old kid on her chest. Exactly like my wife carries the name of our daughter Smadar on hers." Rami made a circle with his fingers and placed them in the center of his chest, where his shirt buttons fastened.

"I'm not a religious person," he said. "I have no way of explaining what happened to me back then. All I can say is that from that moment on, until today, I devoted my life to go everywhere possible, to talk to anyone possible—people who want to listen and people who will not listen—to convey this very basic, very simple message that says, 'We are not doomed.' This is not our destiny to keep on killing each other in this holy land of ours forever. We can change it. We can break, once and for all, the cycle of violence and revenge and retaliation. And the only way to do this is simply by talking to each other. It will not stop unless we talk."

When he said this, I remember clearly noticing the soft lamplight behind him. The way the light had shifted in the room, the way the lamp glowed at that moment. It seemed almost to be crowning his head. Like a halo.

He spoke on. "So I believe that you need to teach yourself how to listen. I believe that once you're able to listen to the pain of the other, you can expect the other to listen to your pain, and only then start this very long journey towards reconciliation, maybe some kind of peace in the end. It's a very long and bumpy road. No shortcuts. This is the only way possible because the other way leads to nowhere. And the price of the other way is really too heavy, too horrible."

Today, over six hundred families make up the Parents Circle. Rami said it's one of the only organizations in the world that does not want new members. And so they plead with their countries for peace.

"We bang our heads against this very high wall of hatred and fear that divides these two nations," Rami said. "And we put cracks in it—cracks of hope—until we will put it down. Because there is no other alternative. The alternative is too painful. And we have an enormous ally on our side, which is the power of our pain. You should know that the power of pain is tremendous. It is very much like nuclear energy. And like this enormous energy, you can use it to bring darkness, destruction, pain, and death to people. And you can use this energy to bring light, warmth, and hope.

"We go around the country and talk to kids in Israeli and Palestinian high schools. Hundreds of meetings. And we tell them our blood is exactly the same color. That our pain is exactly the same pain. And our tears are just as bitter. And if we who paid the highest price possible—if we can talk to each other, then anyone can. Anyone should."

THE FIRST TIME I heard the name Bassam Aramin was in my conversation with Rami. He was talking about the importance of respect in building a lasting peace between Israelis and Palestinians, and so he spoke of a man for whom he has the highest respect. "I wish that Bassam Aramin would be my prime minister, my president, and my king," Rami told me. After sitting with Rami for an hour that Sunday in Jerusalem, I developed a great respect for him, as I'm sure anyone would. So I decided to speak with the man Rami respected most, the man he wished to follow.

I met Bassam in his stone office in Beit Jala, a Palestinian town next to Bethlehem. When he walked in the room, I noticed a prominent limp. I soon learned this came from a bout of childhood polio—the first of the many hardships he had to survive. His face seemed weathered but tender, with tired eyes, like they'd seen too much or wept the tears from which eyes don't fully recover.

Like Rami, Bassam has told his story hundreds, even thousands, of times. I wonder if he ever grows tired of telling it, of talking so much of such difficult things. But still, I asked if he was willing to tell it again.

"It's very difficult to be a Palestinian," was his first sentence. Speaking in what is likely his third or fourth language, Bassam told me of his rural upbringing. "It's a very complicated conflict. Until the age of twelve, I never faced the question of Israelis, Palestinians, Arabs, Jewish—because I was born in a cave very far away from the village. We have our own life. Small family—fifteen brothers and sisters. I don't even know all of them." He hesitated, as a sheepish smile appeared. "I'm joking," he said. I laughed awkwardly, realizing I'd missed the joke. Thankfully, he kept going. "When we moved to the village near Hebron to live there, I start to see very strange soldiers."

Bassam described the brutality of the Israeli soldiers he encountered near Hebron and how even at a young age, he and his friends wanted to fight back. One of the ways they sought to resist the occupation was to raise the Palestinian flag. This was in the early '80s, before the first Palestinian intifada. Bassam told me that flying the Palestinian flag was a crime then. He and his friends knew that the job of the Israeli army at that time was to "follow the flag," removing it from sight wherever it appeared. The problem was, when Bassam's brigade hung the flag from olive trees around the school, the soldiers simply cut down the entire grove. Disproportionate retaliation—an Israeli Defense Forces tactic since the 1950s.

"You start to think as a fighter, as a warrior," he told me. "You see that you have no safe place for yourself, and you want to fight to defend yourself, even as a kid."

At sixteen, Bassam was with his friends when they found some weapons in a cave. Some of them decided to try out their newfound grenades on an Israeli military patrol. Their aim was poor, however, and thankfully no one was injured. Even so, a year later, Bassam and all his friends were arrested for the attack. Bassam had been unable to participate because of his limp, but it didn't matter. For the military, he was guilty by association. His friends received heavy prison sentences: twenty-one years, nineteen years, fifteen years, and fourteen years. Bassam got seven.

While he was in jail, Bassam heard that a documentary about the Holocaust would be on television. He wanted to see it. He didn't believe at that time that the scale of the Holocaust was as massive as everyone said. Perhaps it was a few thousand Jews who died, he thought. Not six million. But Bassam had struggled under military occupation from the Jewish state for most of his life, and now he was in prison. At least, he thought, he could find some satisfaction in watching a film about Jewish suffering.

But it didn't go as he planned. "In a few minutes, I found myself crying. I could not bear that. It's too much." Bassam tried to convince himself that what he saw in the documentary couldn't be real, that humans couldn't be so abhorrent. Despite his skepticism about the truth of the film, a curiosity sprouted. He needed to understand more, especially because it was clear to him that the story of the Holocaust was informing the violence of Israel's soldiers. It was a cycle; what is not transformed is transferred. He realized that it didn't matter if the whole thing were a well-calculated lie. Because if the *soldiers believed* this story of near annihilation, their belief would continue to breed brutality.

Bassam did his best to learn the story. He was told at the time that understanding his enemy was the path to victory. "If you know your enemy, you can defeat him, you can kill him," Bassam said, summarizing this view. "If you only hate him, you will kill yourself. So I have a very clear way that I start to study, to listen to the news, to understand this enemy, to understand the jailers. In jail, we don't talk to the jailers. They see us as terrorists, killers, with blood on our hands, exactly as you hear in the media."

At some point, though, one of the jailers—a man called Hertzl—broke the rules. He began talking with Bassam. "So, once, I have a dialogue with my jailer. He looks at me and is very sorry for me because I am a kid, and he asked me, 'It's not good for you to be a terrorist. Why you are here?'" The two exchanged accusations about who were the true killers, terrorists, liberators, and settlers. Bassam issued Hertzl a challenge: Prove that the Palestinians are, in fact, the illegal settlers in the land and he would swear off violence forever. Hertzl agreed.

And this is how they began to talk, little by little, over days and weeks and months. Over time, Hertzl offered Bassam coffee from a glass instead of the "dreadful plastic cups" the prisoners often used. It was, for Bassam, a small gesture of decency—perhaps even of respect. At the beginning of those conversations with Hertzl, Bassam's position was rigid. "Of course, in that time for me, he had no right to exist. There is no state of Israel. If you want to live, yes, you can live with us in the Palestinian state, exactly as our Jewish brothers lived in the Islamic state."

But these conversations started messing with his certainty. "I discovered later that I change my mind," Bassam said. "I want to accept him." This was a shocking realization. How could he see Hertzl as someone to accept and not as an enemy to conquer?

"But still," Bassam said, "it's only one man. What does that mean?" The fact was, and remains, that for most Palestinians in the West Bank and Gaza, the only Israelis they encounter are carrying weapons, controlling and too often harassing them. For most of these Palestinians, Israelis are known only through the settlers building homes on Palestinian land. Or the soldiers stationed at checkpoints, or invading Palestinian homes, or shooting bullets and gas at clashes, or stopping and searching people, or managing the prison cells. One man, Bassam thought, was just one man. The conflict was so much bigger than that.

Then came October 1, 1987. A day that something terrible happened. In his prison block, there were 120 prisoners, ranging from twelve to nineteen years old. The majority, he told me, were less than sixteen. They were essentially children, with long sentences. One fourteen-year-old friend of Bassam's received a fifteen-year sentence.

"We are waiting for our lunch," Bassam said about that first day of October. "Suddenly, we hear an alarm, and so we enter into our rooms. The alarm takes longer than usual. Always we have this alarm. I was in the last room, number 8, with the people ages eighteen and nineteen. We start to hear crying, shouting. Then we discover that more than one hundred soldiers had entered the section, standing in two lines, going to each room. We must take off our clothes, go back to the corridor, and make our way to a square, and they would beat us from both sides. Naked. When they come to my room," he paused, "we go outside. Everyone is naked, which is . . . I cannot describe how painful it is. Then suddenly, in this atmosphere, they are smiling and laughing and beating us. Like machines. You can see the *kids*—always they come back to me." He moved his hand backward, near his head, showing me he was talking about memories he can't shake.

Though Bassam saw no resistance in his Palestinian comrades, he refused to comply with this abuse. He shouted in every language he knew, hurling furious insults and challenges at the soldiers. The soldiers met his resistance with their own fury and dragged him into a side room to be beaten alone. That's where his story took an unexpected turn.

"In the middle of that," he said, "someone came to lay on me, to protect me with his body." He paused again. "And this was my jailer."

Hertzl. I grunted as the weight of what Bassam had just said settled on me. This was a dangerous move for Hertzl. He risked his own body for the safety of his enemy, the one he had named as a terrorist and a killer. Placing himself between his fellow soldiers and their target took a level of courage that is hard to imagine. No group looks kindly on those they see as traitors.

Bassam told me that Hertzl cried out for them to stop. "And he said, 'No one touch him! He has a problem in his heart. I know him! He will die, and you will be responsible for that.'"

Hertzl moved Bassam to safety, apologized, and left. Later that night, he returned to Bassam's cell and told him that what had happened was not the doings of the jailers; this had been a special military exercise. These soldiers were training, and their training was to beat Palestinian prisoners.

When Bassam was finally released in 1992, the Oslo peace process was underway. Despite his skepticism, he couldn't help but feel some hope and stability. He decided that now, with peace near, it was safe to create a family. He got married and had his first child in 1994.

Fatherhood changed Bassam. The bravado of his youth disappeared. He wanted to set a good example for his son—or at least a safer one. Little by little, he started realizing that all the fighting hadn't really worked. "You start to think that for one hundred years, we try to kill each other. Yet Israel is not safe, Palestine is not free, and we have more blood, more pain, more victims." Bassam was waking up to the idea of nonviolence as a strategy. He was interested in nonviolence not for the sake of his occupiers, but rather for the sake of his own people. Nothing else was working. Perhaps it was time to talk.

In 2002, Bassam learned of a group known as the Israeli "refuseniks." These Israelis recognize the injustice of the military occupation of Palestinian land and people and therefore refuse to serve in occupied Palestine. Bassam could hardly believe it, and he wanted to meet with some of these soldiers to understand why they refused to be part of the occupation. In 2005, his wish came true, and a meeting was arranged.

At a restaurant called Everest, at the top of Beit Jala, Bassam and three other former Palestinian political prisoners waited for the arrival of seven former Israeli officers, including Rami's son Elik. I can only imagine how afraid they all must have been. Bassam and his friends wondered if the Israelis coming might actually be undercover Israeli agents. I imagine the Israelis wondered whether this meeting might be a ruse to lure them into the West Bank to kidnap and murder them. The fear among them was palpable—and so was the courage.

"You can see the fear in their eyes," Bassam remembered. "They served in this area, as soldiers and officers, and today, for the first time, they came without the M16, without the unit, without the tank, and they've come to meet Palestinian 'terrorists.' So it's a real fear; it's not a joke. And every one of them gave his number to a friend: 'If something happens, we will call you.' Yeah, it's not a joke. So you can imagine the first meeting."

In this initial encounter between these former combatants, politics dominated the conversation, but not with the dynamics Bassam expected. The Israelis sitting with him that day agreed with all his political demands: East Jerusalem must be the Palestinian capital, for example, and there should be no settlements. "They agree about everything we say," Bassam told me. "They didn't even give me the chance to fight with them."

That first meeting didn't finish with hugs and warm wishes, though. Bassam said it took a year of meetings to make real progress. But he saw something hopeful in the Israelis he met that day. Bassam began recruiting former political prisoners, men he knew while on the inside, trying to convince them to join the conversations. The power in these meetings, he told me, lay in the discovering of one another. They already knew each other as enemies, but now they could meet each other without the uniforms. They could try to find the common humanity. Discovering that this "war criminal officer" in front of you, the man who represents all you've hated, is also a "very gentle man, a very kind man"—I imagine it would feel devastating. Bassam called it a "disaster." I think that's a perfect word.

I believe narrative is the foundation of everything. There are stories we tell ourselves about ourselves, and there are stories we tell ourselves about others. We build these stories like stones in an arch, one against the other, holding everything up. To go after the narrative is to threaten the whole structure. Yet until the narrative changes, nothing really does.

"Our struggle from the beginning," Bassam said, "is what Nelson Mandela says, 'If you want to defeat your enemy, you need to work with your enemy, and then he becomes your partner.' So from the beginning, I told them, 'We are not friends, we are not brothers, we are not family. We are real enemies.' And especially *us*, the combatants—we did our best to kill each other physically from both sides. So our goal is to be partners.

"And simply, we discover each other," he continued. "That we are people; we are the same. We want to kill each other to achieve peace and security. Of course, each one from his point of view. We understand that there's nothing like 'the truth'; each one has his own truth. I start to learn the other side. And then I start to see the soldiers in the checkpoints not as targets. For the first time, I start to look at their faces and think, 'This one is like Michael, this one is like Zohar.' They have faces. Nothing changed in one way; the occupation is still there. But the change starts in yourself. If you are familiar with Rumi, he said that, 'Yesterday I am clever, so I start to change the world. Today I am wise, so I start to change myself.' Just change yourself and you will change the world—*your* world. That's it. You will see things differently."

All these conversations with former Israeli soldiers led to the creation of Combatants for Peace, an organization that believes the one-hundred-year violence of the conflict will end only when Israelis and Palestinians join forces on a foundation of nonviolence. This part of Bassam's story is filled with hope.

Then he told me about January 16, 2007. He left long pauses between sentences as he spoke. "It's unbelievable. It's a very normal day, very normal day—no demonstrations. At nine-thirty in the morning, my children left for their school, to finish their exams. The jeep crossed them... It was one bullet, a rubber bullet, one—that's it. She fell down. And two days later, she passed away." His daughter Abir had been shot and killed by an Israeli soldier while she was walking out of a candy shop. She was ten years old.

Bassam walked me through the aftermath of the gunshot. The soldier's rubber bullet struck Abir in the back of the head. She fell to the ground outside the shop on a street corner. People swarmed to her aid, carefully lifted her body, and placed her in a car. The car sped the winding roads toward Makassed Hospital, a Palestinian medical center in East Jerusalem. By the time a frantic Bassam and his wife, Salwa, arrived at the hospital, Abir's condition was grim. Bassam's friend was a nurse at the hospital.

"I spoke to him directly," Bassam told me, "and said, 'What's the situation?' And he said, 'You are my brother. Prepare yourself.'" Bassam paused, remembering. "Just like that: 'Prepare yourself.' It means, prepare yourself for the worst."

At the hospital, Bassam learned that Abir would need immediate surgery. So he told the hospital staff to move her to Hadassah, a top-rate hospital nearby in West Jerusalem. Israel's healthcare is among the finest in the world. His daughter's life hung in the balance; they couldn't take any chances. Abir needed the best care available if she were to survive. The transfer to Hadassah should have been quick, but it took three hours. "Every moment," he said, "you could write a book about it."

When they finally arrived at Hadassah, Rami and Nurit were there to meet them. "Then one hour later," Bassam told me, "more than thirty Israeli families come and stay with me two days hoping Abir will wake. This was unbearable for me."

But Abir didn't wake. She died there at the hospital.

Bassam, like Rami, knew the choice he had to make: the work of building peace had to continue. "Because simply, I have another five kids," he said. "They deserve to live. We need to protect our kids, not kill them. And I don't ask for revenge, because there is no revenge, in fact. You will never meet your daughter again, and it will not ease your pain, even to kill the rest of the world."

For four and a half years, the Israeli courts opened and closed the case of Abir's death repeatedly, sending Bassam's family on a roller coaster. In the end, as Bassam expected, the Israeli Supreme Court officially closed the case, citing insufficient evidence to convict. However, during a court appearance for Abir's case, Bassam met the man who murdered his daughter. So he spoke to him.

"I told him, 'I need you to know that you are not a hero; you are not a warrior. You did not kill the enemy or the terrorist. You just killed a ten-year-old girl in her head from the back. And if you think it's okay to kill my daughter, enjoy your crime. I don't take revenge from victims. You are the real victim, not my daughter.' And he didn't expect to hear something like this from an Arab savage, a terrorist. I told him, 'If any day in your life, you want to recognize that you committed a crime, you did something wrong, you harmed somebody, and you want to find me to forgive you, always I will be there. I will forgive you. But not because of yourself. It's because of myself. Because I love my daughter very much and because I have another five kids. And I don't want us to be your victims.'

"Two months later," Bassam continued, "I meet him again in the same court. And you can see the change, of course. Because he's a human being and not a serial killer. He recognized that he killed a kid, a peace activist, who has tears, who has a heart, exactly like him. He didn't have the courage to look at me and my wife. And always I told him, 'Come to us to forgive you. I want to forgive you.'"

"So today, he still has not come to you?" I asked.

"One day he will come," Bassam said. "I promise you. He will come. And when he comes, I will forgive him."

IN MARK 8, the storyteller says Jesus met a man in Bethsaida who was blind, but Jesus didn't heal him immediately. Jesus takes him outside the village and spits in his eyes. But his sight isn't restored right away. Not fully. The man can see only bits and pieces. Everything is blurry. "The people look like trees," he tells Jesus. Fuzzy. Unclear. So Jesus touches his eyes again. This time the man can see everything. The writer of Mark says the man "looked with eyes wide open."

Bassam and Rami see with eyes wide open. They know the truth of the world. They see the possibility of it. And we must too. The man from Bethsaida had his eyes opened by a wandering teacher from Galilee. For some, our eyes might be opened by suffering, oppression, and bereavement. For others, proximity to people in pain. And for others, stories. However it happens, sooner or later, we all must awake. We must wash away the scales, like the apostle Paul after the Damascus Road. We must look with eyes wide open.

Change comes in the steps. It's true. But this is not an excuse for laziness. Nor for apathy. We cannot sit with hands folded and do nothing, Abdullah Awwad told me in his paradise. We have to *work* for peace. We must *choose* to take the steps that lead to change. Like Rami. Like Bassam.

Remarkably, after all Bassam suffered at the hands of the Israeli state—childhood traumas, incarceration, beatings, a murdered child—he still went to graduate school in peace studies and focused on the Jewish Holocaust. He wanted to understand more deeply the stories and suffering of the neighbors he once saw only as enemies. After all, he said to me, it was *one* Israeli soldier who killed his daughter but *one hundred* former soldiers who came to his village to build a playground honoring the child he had to bury.

Change comes in steps. So we must walk.

TODAY, RAMI IS THE ISRAELI LEADER and Bassam the Palestinian leader for the Parents Circle-Families Forum. Both men lost what is unbearable to lose. Rami is a former Israeli soldier whose daughter was murdered by a Palestinian combatant. Bassam is a former Palestinian combatant whose daughter was murdered by an Israeli soldier. In the world of war, these two have every reason to hate each other. Their grief could drive them toward vengeance.

But their eighth day came, as it comes for us all. Shiva ends. Everyone goes home. We are left with our grief and a decision: What will we do with our pain? This question is where Rami and Bassam live their lives now. Day after day, they choose again. And instead of reaching for a gun, they reach for one another.

Theirs are stories that might save us. Like all the stories I met along the way, Rami and Bassam's tell me that in the violence of conflict, we may well have every reason to hate each other. Because enemies do exist, fear is real, and the worst pain we can imagine may find us at any time.

And their stories tell me that we can find a way out. That we can do better than a world with enemies. That courage can accompany fear. And that the worst pain we can imagine has the possibility of leading us to a world beyond violence.

With Ali, we can use dialogue as a carrier to freedom for all people.

With Dr. Zoughbi, we can come alongside each other in the ongoing traumas of our lives.

With Moran, we can tend to what is wounded.

With Robi, we can refuse to seek vengeance from our pain.

With Abdullah and Al Basma, we can create paradise through our hospitality and love for the beauty that's been pushed to the margins.

With Corrymeela, we can be a haven for those needing refuge, a shelter for story, and a way station through life's lumpy crossings.

With Jo, we can make space within ourselves for even the story of our enemy.

With Eleanor, we can cast out the demons of oppression that curse us all, in one way or another.

With Themba, we can rid the poisons of hatred within us and those of injustice around us.

And with Rami and Bassam, we can greet our grieving with a determination to save other people from our pain.

We can ram our heads against the walls that divide us, until we put cracks in them—cracks of hope.

ACKNOWLEDGMENTS

First and foremost, I must thank all the people I interviewed for sharing their time, stories, and trust with me. I sincerely hope this book honors the gifts you gave me.

Thank you also to the organizations that partnered with me: Combatants for Peace, the Parents Circle, the Corrymeela Community, the Institute for Justice and Reconciliation, and the Desmond and Leah Tutu Foundation. I would never have met the incredible people I spoke with had it not been for your generosity.

My deepest thanks to the International Services office at Texas Christian University—and specifically Ed McNertney, James English, and John Singleton—for approving the funding for this project back in 2015, providing support, trusting me to work well with TCU students, and connecting me to the amazing faculty partners to whom I'm most grateful: Drs. Rima Abunasser, Mark Dennis, and Ralph Carter.

I would not have been able to meet my manuscript deadline had it not been for all those who transcribed the hours of interviews: Anna McRay, Claire Brown, Zac Swann, John Herron, Chuck Beard, Craig Katzenmiller, Hamzah Raza, Carter Hannah, and Sue-Jin Green. Y'all were lifesavers.

Christy Lynch, your editing vision on my book proposal was a true help. Glad you could spare two eyes.

To my literary agent, Angela Scheff—my sincerest thanks for opening doors I couldn't open on my own. I'm overjoyed Shane connected us. My gratitude to you for putting my proposal in the hands of Herald Press and staying my advocate along the way.

To the good people of Herald Press, particularly my editors Valerie Weaver-Zercher, Sara Versluis, and Meghan Florian—I am deeply thankful for your belief in this project and for taking the chance on an unknown author like me. Also, Reuben Graham, the book cover is stunning. Truly. Thank you so much for your creative brilliance in designing it.

To Ishmael Beah, I cannot thank you enough for supporting this book with a foreword. I have such respect for you, and I'm honored you added your voice to all the voices in these pages.

My utmost gratitude to all the endorsers who made time amidst such full schedules to read and blurb the book. You are all inspirations to me.

To Lisa Consiglio and my colleagues at Narrative 4, I offer sincere thanks for giving me some time off to finish writing this, and for all the support you've offered in allowing me to travel and promote it.

Mom and Dad, my gratitude and love to you as always for your unwavering support and pride. So much of this book became possible because of the lessons you've taught and the love you instilled in me for travel, stories, and social justice.

To all my friends whom I've disappointed as I've worked on this, I am sorry. Thank you for not abandoning me forever and having patience with me as I finished the book. I'm free for a drink now.

And to my love, Brittany—you have been a rock. I left to pursue this project one month after we started dating. And now, five years later, the book has finally arrived. Your constant support, affirmations, proofreading, patience, and cooking more than your fair share of dinners has carried me through this. I don't know how I could have done this without you. I love you.

P.S. If I left anyone out, I apologize, and I'll give you a free book as penance.

SUGGESTED READING

Alexander, Michelle. *The New Jim Crow: Mass Incarceration in the Age of Colorblindness*. 2nd ed. New York: The New Press, 2012.

Beah, Ishmael. *A Long Way Gone: Memoirs of a Boy Soldier*. New York: Sarah Crichton Books, 2007.

Coates, Ta-Nehisi. *Between the World and Me*. New York: Spiegel and Grau, 2015.

DiAngelo, Robin. *White Fragility: Why It's So Hard for White People to Talk about Racism*. Boston: Beacon Press, 2018.

du Toit, Fanie, and Erik Doxtader, eds. *In the Balance: South Africans Debate Reconciliation*. Auckland Park, SA: Jacana Media, 2011.

Equal Justice Initiative. *Lynching in America: Confronting the Legacy of Racial Terror*. 3rd ed. Montgomery, AL: Equal Justice Initiative, 2017. https://lynchinginamerica.eji.org/report/.

Helmick, Raymond G., and Rodney L. Petersen. *Forgiveness and Reconciliation: Religion, Public Policy, and Conflict Transformation*. Philadelphia: Templeton Foundation Press, 2001.

Kendi, Ibram. *Stamped from the Beginning: The Definitive History of Racist Ideas in America*. New York: Nation Books, 2016.

Lederach, John Paul. *The Moral Imagination: The Art and Soul of Building Peace*. New York: Oxford University Press, 2005.

Liechty, Joe, and Cecilia Clegg. *Moving Beyond Sectarianism: Religion, Conflict, and Reconciliation in Northern Ireland*. Dublin: The Columba Press, 2001.

McCann, Colum. *Apeirogon: A Novel*. New York: Random House, 2020.

McRay, Michael T. *Letters from "Apartheid Street": A Christian Peacemaker in Occupied Palestine*. Eugene, OR: Cascade Books, 2013.

———. *Where the River Bends: Considering Forgiveness in the Lives of Prisoners*. Eugene, OR: Cascade Books, 2015.

Munayer, Salim, and Lisa Loden. *Through My Enemy's Eyes: Envisioning Reconciliation in Israel-Palestine*. Carlisle: Paternoster Press, 2014.

Ó Tuama, Pádraig. *In the Shelter: Finding a Home in the World*. London: Hodder and Stoughton, 2015.

Olson, Pamela J. *Fast Times in Palestine: A Love Affair with a Homeless Homeland*. Berkeley, CA: Seal Press, 2013.

Shehadeh, Raja. *Palestinian Walks: Forays Into a Vanishing Landscape*. New York: Scribner, 2007.

Tutu, Desmond. *No Future Without Forgiveness*. London: Rider, 1999.

THE AUTHOR

Michael T. McRay is a writer, facilitator, story-practitioner, and the author of two previous books: *Where the River Bends* and *Letters from "Apartheid Street."* He's also the co-editor of *Keep Watch with Me: An Advent Reader for Peacemakers.* McRay works often with the global nonprofit Narrative 4, which builds empathy through personal story exchanges. He founded and hosts the public monthly storytelling night Tenx9 Nashville, occasionally teaches at Lipscomb University, leads narrative retreats, and speaks on story, conflict, reconciliation, and forgiveness. McRay has a master's degree in conflict resolution and reconciliation from Trinity College Dublin's Belfast campus. He lives in Nashville, Tennessee, with his wife, Brittany, where they will soon welcome their first child, Rowan. Connect with him @michaeltmcray on Instagram and Facebook or at MichaelMcRay.com.

For an interview with the author and a guide for group discussion on the book, subscribe to www.MichaelMcRay.com.